T0114815

More Than We Imagine

Stories of a Living Hope

CARA WALTER

WESTBOW
PRESS®
A DIVISION OF THOMAS NELSON
& ZONDERVAN

WestBow Press books may be ordered through booksellers or by contacting:

WestBow Press
A Division of Thomas Nelson & Zondervan
1663 Liberty Drive
Bloomington, IN 47403
www.westbowpress.com
844-714-3454

Author photo by Jennifer Lee

ISBN: 978-1-6642-2295-3 (sc)
ISBN: 978-1-6642-2294-6 (e)

Print information available on the last page.

WestBow Press rev. date: 02/16/2021

CONTENTS

Acknowledgements..vii

Dedication ix

Opening   First Things First...1

Chapter 1   A Love to Break Through All Barriers 11

Chapter 2   Created for Purpose 23

Chapter 3   An Education on Discernment.............................37

Chapter 4   More Than Enough 49

Chapter 5   He Makes Things New..63

Chapter 6   Doing Life With Jesus 77

Chapter 7   Prepared for Battle...95

Closing   Your Turn 111

References 117

About the Author..119

ACKNOWLEDGEMENTS

I am beyond humbled and grateful for all of the love and support showered over my life, especially during the last few years. Transitions are never easy, and for a woman who likes plans and checklists, the great span of "in-between" would have overwhelmed me if not for each of you!

To my incredible husband, partner, best friend and soul mate, Tim: Thank you for loving me so well! Hardworking, generous, loyal, kind, and the funniest man on the planet, I have never doubted that we're in this together (no matter how many months we were apart), and I can't WAIT to see how we'll continue to grow and complement one another in this next season.

To Patrick and Evan, the two young men who gave me some of life's greatest lessons: It has been my utmost joy and privilege to be your Mom! Thank you for continuing to share your lives with me even as you have grown and followed your own paths. I know that Abba has great designs on each of you.

To my dearest friends who amaze me with ongoing encouragement: Thank you Kelly for your prayers, your spiritual insights, and your remarkable friendship that continued to develop though we were thousands of miles apart for years. You are the epitome of connection and strength and you truly carry His Peace with you, sharing it with others as you warm every environment you enter.

Thank you Joeke for partnering with me to help make it possible to share my gifts in this transitional time. Your championing of my speaking and your incredibly solid faith gave me such courage in this season of "unknown future." You are a true friend and though we'll now be separated by miles, I look forward to years of adventures with you, Wise Woman.

To my new friend Peggy, a woman of both beautiful Southern charm and solid godly accountability: Thank you for not only reading the first draft of this manuscript—providing kind encouragement and helpful probing questions—but especially for offering me a lifeline during this season of Covid isolation. You gave me a sense of belonging in a time that could have been incredibly lonely.

To my Pop, Skip, and wonderful bonus mom, Betty: Thank you for so quickly and so completely welcoming us as family! You are proof that our Hope is real, that restoration comes, and that healthy parent-child bonds are both possible and beautiful at any age. Knowing you has changed our lives for the better.

And finally, with special thanks to the wonderful people who helped me get this book ready for publication: my extraordinary editor/beautiful cousin, Suzy, and the team at WestBow Press.

DEDICATION

For my Abba/Jesus/Holy Spirit, the One who literally fills me with AWE and unmitigated JOY: It is because of You that all of the preceding relationships exist. You are Love and Life itself! Thank You for your perfect timing, for divine appointments and glorious manifestations, for your boundless mercy, instruction, provision, and favor. I eagerly anticipate our face-to-face encounters to come, when I am finally, fully the woman You created me to be.

OPENING

First Things First

I have come to give you everything in abundance,
more than you expect—life in its fullness until you
overflow. (John 10:10 TPT)

Once Upon a Time…
I have always loved a good story. Books allowed me to explore vastly different lives, witness battles between good and evil, thrill to the blush of first love, join my favorite detective in solving mysteries, and laugh out loud over the comical antics of favorite characters. Words have a way of creating vivid pictures in my imagination, and while I might not ever remember plot points, certain colorfully described episodes from stories read long ago still remain etched in my memory today.

And what about story time itself? I came from a home where reading was the norm. When I was little, books were shared with my brother and me not just at bedtime, but at any time of day. A rainy afternoon… when siblings squabbled over a toy… to provide my mother a little break from the tedium of laundry and housework, stories always seemed the perfect solution. When I look back it's not such a surprise that I was reading before I entered kindergarten. To this day I would argue that <u>my</u> mom had the best pillow-like upper arms as we snuggled together over our favorite books.

Maybe story time means something else to you... Did you have a favorite elementary school teacher who would let you put your head down on your desk after recess as she read another chapter from the class novel? I remember the cool of the desk against my cheek as eyes closed, I imagined myself right there with Scout in her turnip costume, or with the gang in the barnyard celebrating Charlotte's latest web to save "Some Pig."[i] I remember how comforting it was to be able to shut out the troubles at home, or the mean girls' latest bullying.

Through the years my connection to the world of story continued and developed. I wrote a few, mostly tragic tales during the angst of my teen years, and then in college I learned how to adapt literature for performance. Later I became the parent who loved reading to my own sons at bedtime, and for a season, the classroom teacher who read to my students after lunch recess. I still take paperback books with me on beach vacations, and until moving recently, one of my all-time favorite volunteer positions has been as a narrator of talking books for the WTBBL (Washington Talking Book and Braille Library).

This background information is important for one reason only— it demonstrates a wealth of input and experience for comparison when I say, I've read many, many wonderfully inspiring stories, but nothing, NOTHING has impacted my life like "The Greatest Story Ever Told." The irony of course is that it would be years before I actually understood what I was reading whenever I attempted to crack open the Bible. *Ok, I could follow the story of Noah's Ark, or Jonah getting swallowed by a big fish, but most of what I read was so violent, or to be frank, so boring to me that I just put it down.* It also didn't help that the people I knew who talked a lot about their religion were so legalistic as to be a real turnoff. Hear me on this one, that's not God's Book at all—from cover to cover the Bible is a love story. What I finally learned was that you have to have spiritual eyes to understand it. My journey into His Word formally began once I became a follower of Jesus—

That's a story in itself!

Just after I turned 3, my parents took my brother and me to a "family friendly" Super Bowl party that would ultimately start me on a trajectory of life-changing importance. The grown-ups were all in the large living room—cheering for their team, drinking beer and the like—while the kids played together in another part of the home, so as not to disturb the game. What can I say? This was the 60's. There wasn't much child supervision at these kinds of events back then. Fortunately for us however, the adult intruder who joined our little kid party wasn't a predator, but rather, *as my mom called her*, the "Bible-thumper." Mim told us stories about a baby Jesus who came to save the world and then my brother, my forever friend, Stacey, and I all got on our knees as Mim led us through a prayer asking Jesus to come into our hearts. A sweet memory to be sure, followed up with a few years of Sunday school (my parents dropped us off in the mornings and then went out for breakfast), but this was merely a shadow of things to come. A seed that has no water or sunlight doesn't grow roots. I had just enough Sunday school as a child to be familiar with the rudimentary facts of Christianity. For years I even thought I was a Christian without ever making any kind of real commitment. *A little bit of head knowledge in any area can be a dangerous thing when we don't dig in deeper to investigate.*

In college I developed close friendships with two students who were deeply committed to their faith and who continued to follow their religious traditions despite it being a difficult thing to do on a secular college campus. One was Catholic, the other was Jewish, and I became a seeker. By this point in my life I wanted a genuine faith too! My childhood had been difficult; with fears of abandonment, and having assimilated the lie that I would never "fit in," I found the idea of God looking out after me very inviting, if somewhat confusing. However once again, without any consistent shepherding, the notion became dormant.

As I look back, I can see how Jesus pursued me for years. I majored in theatre in college and joined a professional acting company after graduation. Guess who frequently was cast in roles where the character was religious? You guessed it. See, Jesus knew I'd do my homework. And He was so faithful, even when I stopped seeking God and started following worldly trends. Choosing to be my own boss meant that I would make many stupid mistakes all the way through my 20's, but still Jesus rescued me from myself. Once He literally saved my life (and limb) in a horrific car accident. I'll be talking more about this in Chapter 2, but for now I'll just say, at the time it was enough for me to start believing that there really was a "force" for good out there who saved me, and therefore, maybe my life had meaning.

When I was 32 my husband wanted us to start going to church as a family; our three-year-old son knew all about Santa Claus and the Easter Bunny, but he didn't know about Jesus. I was really up for it too. By this time I was teaching Language Arts and Math in a Jewish Day School, and the spiritual traditions I saw in my students' families once again ignited the spark in me that was searching for a real faith. Finally, it was during this period when we began regularly going to a church with solid Bible teaching and inspiring worship music, that things began to change. We bought study Bibles and began to read the Word at home. We also began reading the <u>Left Behind</u> books[ii], popular enough at the time that this Christian fictional series ended up on pallets at Costco! No doubt about it, I was THIRSTY, and sure enough– Jesus was waiting for me.

I don't remember the actual message series that was being preached, but for weeks the Pastor offered an altar call for all who wanted a real, life-saving relationship with Christ. Every week I bowed my head and prayed for Him to be my Savior. I meant it. I believed it. Yet I didn't feel any different. (Sometimes we're a bit stubborn at 32.) Then one night I heard **The Voice.** "Get up." Let me tell you, I scrambled out of the blankets so fast I rocked the waterbed and woke my husband! "It's ok," I said, kneeling at the side of the bed. "Go back to sleep. I'm being saved over here!" And that was it!! While there would be many MANY steps and lessons along the journey, my foundation was solid. From that moment on, I KNEW I was the real thing—a beloved child of God!

As my faith has grown so has my experience of His Presence. Later I'll be sharing stories of sightings, how and what I hear from Him, and even the incredible ways He has reached into the natural world to hold me. This can happen for YOU too! However, like every good gift that comes from God, you have to BELIEVE and RECEIVE. This is easier for some than others; for me—with my baggage—it took years. Yet I don't regret a minute of this exquisite journey into God's heart; I am more excited about life, more fully ALIVE than I ever thought possible!

How about you? I'm not asking you if you're a thrill seeker or a couch potato; this isn't about what fascinating thing you do for a living or about how many people share a residence with you who occasionally create chaos. Simply put, do you wake up most mornings with an eager anticipation of the day ahead? Do you sometimes find yourself literally bubbling over with joy? Are you surprised by your own courage in the face of what used to make you insecure? If, as you're reading this, you're thinking "no," "not lately" or "not usually," maybe this is your wake-up call! What if God Himself set up the circumstances just so—so that today, at this very moment, YOU would "just happen" to find this and begin to read? Imagine it: God, the Creator of the universe, the One who set this little blue planet in orbit around a medium-sized star, exactly where it needed to be in order to sustain life, the One who imagined hearts and brains and connective tissue and bone, and then breathed life into being, the One who crafted majestic mountain peaks, white sand beaches along tropical turquoise waters, and deep green leafy foliage under a canopy of towering forest trees… Just imagine that this Almighty God planned for you to be born at the exact time and place in history where you might grow into exactly the kind of curious person who at this very minute is open to a breathtaking possibility? What if God set this moment up because His greatest desire is to know YOU personally? Following Christ and getting to know Him doesn't happen only on Sundays. It's a journey meant to change your entire life! *And trust me, even if you haven't yet made a decision about Jesus, we all believe in something.* Faith is what gives meaning to the past, sustains the present, and imagines the future.

So let's get real—there's not a person on the planet who didn't grow up dreaming of living an exciting big life someday. Not one child is ever born who expects the happy times to be anemic, the sad times long and punishing, and most of his or her life to simply roll along in ho-hum boredom with an endless to-do list. Why would we? We were all designed for love, adventure, and fulfilment. We were born with emotions so rich that we could weep over beauty and take delight in challenges. And yet, how many of us truly reach the heights and depths of our own feelings? I recently lost an old college friend who fought hard to hang onto his life. Reminiscent of the country song, "Live Like You Were Dying"[iii], he came to a place of tender reflection where he appreciated the little things and loved with all his might. My question is—why don't we live like we're LIVING?

Jesus said, "I have come to give you everything in abundance, more than you expect—life in its fullness until you overflow!" (John 10:10 TPT). Is this YOUR experience? Look at those phrases again: Everything in ABUNDANCE, MORE than you expect, life in its FULLNESS. That's the life I want to live; don't YOU? It saddens me when instead, so many people, (and other Christians especially) talk about "getting by." *I just need to make it to the weekend... We're fine... Work is ok...* And the dreaded, *It is what it is.* Does that sound like Living to you? When did the image bearers of God, temples of the Holy Spirit—created to create and explore and discover—when did we begin to believe that Life was not about thriving and growing and becoming, but rather basic survival? Make no mistake—we're talking about life or death stuff here!

Time for an honest gut check—Don't you know, really Know, deep down in the center of your being that you were made for more? You can feel it, right? You are one of a kind—special, with a unique personality, set of skills, and some deeper understanding that needs to be shared with the world. You were created to make something ... give something... do something that no one else on the planet can do!! We have to stop listening to the dull lifeless lies that say it's ok to be content with *it is what it is*...! I was talking with a young woman this morning who said, "it just means, we accept things the way they are." "No," I was rather insistent, "it means we have given up on expecting things to be the way they are supposed to be."

If all of this is stirring something in you—maybe it's been a while since you felt the fire, or maybe you're like I was and you know ABOUT Jesus, but you don't know Him personally—Accept the invitation! Jesus loves you, yes YOU, more than you can even imagine! It's my joy and privilege to welcome you to the ride of a lifetime!!

By now you might be thinking, "Ok, but why should I listen to you?" And you're right; in the world I'm nobody special, with no special theological education or advanced degrees. I'm not famous or wealthy, technically savvy or socially well-connected. My childhood was troubled, I acted as my own mini-god until I was in my 30's, and I struggled believing that I belonged anywhere. But in spite of my early mess I know today in the core of my being I am God's chosen, cherished, and adored child—and so are YOU! In fact, this book is about how our God is still actively pursuing and tenderly caring for each one of us! I have personally witnessed how He redeems and restores, forgives and provides, protects, and pours out favor like nobody's business on regular people like me! In the nearly 25 years since I put my faith in Jesus, He has instructed me through Bible Study, called me into a unique performance ministry, and healed me from depression and the emotional wounds I've carried since childhood. I have experienced being rescued firsthand in the natural realm, and I have been trained to partner with Him in the spiritual realm. I'll be sharing about all of these things in greater detail in the chapters that follow, but the important thing to note here is that although on my own I have no special qualifications, to our Father, I am incredibly special. Does this sound like your walk with Jesus? *Do you want it to be?*

Keep your mind open to Wonder. As much as you may want to jump to quick assumptions questioning my sanity, resist dismissing these ideas as simply fantasy before you take the time to reflect. We're talking about spiritual things here, not the stuff of the world. Don't resort to mankind's reasoning or wriggle out of the possibility of a miracle.

Once I was with a good friend when a series of fun surprises occurred that were too numerous and too specific to be random. I shared about how they demonstrated God's delight in her and how He was actively engaged in showing Himself in her life. Yet she refused to acknowledge the possibility, preferring to call it "coincidence". Sadly, throughout the ages people with limited or frightened worldviews have worked really hard to convince the rest of us that there is no God. Fighting to control the unexplainable and unknown, they try to explain away miracles and even hard evidence with unprovable (and therefore unscientific) "science." See, if their beliefs about life and death, God and man, evolution, purpose, heaven and hell are wrong, well, then they might have to accept the idea of a Creator. And if there really is a Supreme Being who created the universe and everything in it, then they might have to obey Him. True faith isn't about the need for proof or rational explanations, but if you are someone having trouble with the notion of giving up "coincidences," "chance happenings," and "random" life-altering blessings, you might check out Lee Stroble's The Case for Christ,[iv] or C.S. Lewis' Mere Christianity.[v]

All I can say for sure is that I'm sharing now, as best I can, *and trusting the Holy Spirit for all that I can't* because it's time. I have restarted this book project over and over, put it on a shelf and taken it down again. Ever been passionate about something but something else always seems to get in the way? *We'll be talking about that later too.* Here's the thing, even before the pandemic of 2020, in a world spinning on fear and misinformation, people have been looking for answers, desperate for hope and comfort. Unfortunately, the things we have counted on in the past—trustworthy leadership, unbiased news, financial security, educational pursuits, or even our physical and mental health—have all failed us at some level. But this book isn't about all of that. We've all seen and heard enough; problems don't get better by rehashing them in our minds over and over. I'm not advocating that we become ostriches sticking our heads in the sand. Rather, it's time to look **up**! This is our challenge—to embrace the fullness of the life Jesus promises in a world that wants us to feel hopeless and small.

The stories that are about to follow are true. I know, because they happened to me! I hope you find them to be as inspirational as I do.

One small suggestion as you begin: Take some time for yourself—away from what the media, and from what the people around you are saying is so urgent. Breathe. Stretch. The problems will keep for later. You can expect that there will be all kinds of distractions trying to keep you from reading this, but there will be great reward if you hang in there. (Hey—If you've stuck with me this long, this is for YOU!!) Imagine putting your head down on your school desk once more, ready to listen to your favorite teacher. See yourself curling up into your Dad's lap, or resting your head against your mom's wonderfully soft upper arm. It's story time! Here we go…

CHAPTER 1

A Love to Break Through All Barriers

May you have the power to understand, as all God's people should, how wide, how long, how high, and how deep his love is. May you experience the love of Christ, though it is too great to understand fully. **Then you will be made complete with all the fullness of life and power that comes from God.** (Eph 3:18-19 NLT)

L ittle hairs stood up on the back of my neck as I walked under the vine covered arbor toward the nearly hidden oak door. I had been here before! Although clearly overgrown and in need of some caring attention, there was something so charming, so welcoming about this entrance. I could imagine my boys being entranced by visiting here too. A hidden gem "in the woods," right off the main street, it was like traveling back in time or into a fairy tale. A small sign hung over the little bell that would signal the occupants inside, "Welcome, Friends." Suddenly I realized, this was My handwriting!

The door swung open and I nearly burst out laughing; no wonder that little walkway had seemed so familiar—this was the back entrance to my house. Funny though, I didn't remember that my home had extended all the way to the next street over...

Making my way down one corridor and then another, I was amazed at each new discovery! There was a theatre room and a home gym and a large room—just for crafting. A glassed-in playroom lay just beyond a window, where friends/fellow parents could relax on sofas and converse while still keeping an eye on the kiddoes. It was mind-blowing, just thinking about what such a life could be like. Still, it was also vaguely familiar—like we had seen glimpses of these rooms on the real estate tour when we bought the house, but somehow we had forgotten. Every space was beautifully appointed and furnished, but I noticed they were covered with a thin layer of dust from disuse. *So, they needed attention*, I thought, *but what a prize to reclaim!* Then I came to a grand staircase that led to another large open hallway and decided to climb it. Once again, I discovered a forgotten suite of rooms—this was a master like no other. A beautifully decorated bedroom with an enormous walk-in closet... a luxurious bathroom with a large jetted tub and a shower large enough for two... a private sitting room with a fireplace and French doors leading onto a balcony... I noticed that the hardwood floors could use a polishing, the silver picture frames had begun to tarnish, and I could write my name in the dust on the fireplace mantle. There would be work to do, but I couldn't wait to begin using these rooms! Excitedly I ran out onto the balcony and there was still more! The grounds included a great lawn for family games, a flower garden, a vegetable garden, even a tennis court and swimming pool! Overjoyed by the sheer vastness of it, I was eager to share it with my husband and our sons, reminding them of how we had been blessed. I called out to my husband, "Tim! Tim! You've got to see this!"

That's when I woke up.

This wasn't the first time I had one of these dreams. Over and over again they came in the night. Until now, though there were variations, they always followed the same pattern. The dream always began with me walking through my house, *though it never looked like my actual home*! In the dream, I would always be walking through the familiar surroundings when I'd be surprised by an unexpected door. Sometimes I'd open the door and find a beautiful room all furnished with expensive looking furniture—but other times it would be an entire forgotten wing where I'd find one room leading to another and then another! Sometimes I'd open a door to find a stairway leading to a whole new floor, and sometimes, as I explored, I would come to realize that I actually lived in a huge estate with multiple outbuildings and an unbelievable view of the ocean! This went on for weeks. One common element to these dreams was that every time, whatever was behind the door felt familiar, yet long-forgotten; every room was furnished beautifully yet covered in a layer of dust, and a lot of things needed repairs! But every time I was also thrilled and excited about the discovery and I couldn't wait to reclaim this space. Each time I had these dreams I was startled awake with this urgency and excitement. Once, I was so convinced it was real, I woke up my husband to ask him if he remembered the suite of rooms behind the crawlspace door. Well, he didn't, and he promptly went back to sleep.

Now I don't live in a mansion, and until I join my Father in heaven it's unlikely I will, but this time I finally understood what God was showing me—spiritually speaking I had settled for living my life in a tiny corner bedroom and depression had set in—but God wanted me to have the whole estate!!

Dreams were a part of my emotional healing process, but as is true with just about everything the Lord gives us, they would expand with far richer meaning over time. Can you see how this dream would come back to me in a year where I learned about God's amazing abundance? Remember: Jesus said He came to give us life in its fullness until we overflow! However, the key to experiencing the abundant life He promises each of us is that it only comes once we can finally fully receive His Love. *May you experience the love of Christ, though it is too great to understand fully.* **Then you will be made complete with all the fullness of life and power that comes from God.** (Eph 3: 19 NLT)

From the very beginning of my story Jesus was there with me—pursuing, guiding, and yet waiting for me to invite Him into all of the areas of my life. While He is everything we see in the Bible—our Healer, Master Teacher, Rescuer, and Coming King—He is also a Gentleman. He will woo and challenge, protect and provide, but He will not force Himself on mankind. He can't. Love isn't love unless it's given and received freely. Sadly, for many of us, the ability to believe and accept the unconditional, all-encompassing love of Christ can sometimes be the biggest hurdle to overcome in our walk with Him.

For a few years after my conversion, although I believed in my head what I was learning about Jesus, it was much harder to "get it" in my heart, and I held back some of me in reservation. I mean, I knew that Jesus loved me in a pat-me-on-the-head kind of way, but love that's described as wide and long and high and deep[vi]—well that was for other people, not for me. My childhood was marked with enormous loss and mixed messages. If the people who were supposed to love me best weren't safe, then how could I expect anyone else to care for me deeply? Instead, I believed the lie—I was "too odd," "too different" to be truly loved. The best I could hope for was a superficial, generalized sort of love as one might have for a group of people. Wearing shame like a blanket I believed that individually, I was unworthy of love.

Eventually the gap between my head knowledge and my emotional feelings kicked into high gear and I needed help and healing. Understand, up until this point I was absolutely a faithful follower! I had thrown myself headfirst into Bible study, I was already actively involved in ministry, and I eagerly began sharing the spiritual truths that I was learning as I prayed earnestly each day to become a woman after God's own heart. But until I could shake the lie—believing that in some fundamental way I was unloveable—I had no idea how rich this life was meant to be or how I could fully partner with Him, becoming the woman He designed me to be. My life completely transformed when I finally realized deep in my spirit that Jesus REALLY LOVED ME…

It all began with a serious bout of depression. *I will be forever grateful for it; what the enemy uses to destroy, God can use for good!!* Anyway, I had been seeing a counselor for a few months and I was also in a women's support group focused on emotional healing. Honestly, there was a lot of baggage, childhood trauma, and layers upon layers of denial to break through before any real healing could begin. Some days I barely got off the couch. Some days Depression's ugly sidekick, Anxiety, propelled me into bursts of (mostly unfocused) projects. On this day, something shifted in my spirit. My counselor was talking me through a visualization exercise; our first target would be the lie that I was too weird or odd to be loved.

"Look down at your feet. There's a rock there named 'Odd'. Do you see it?" *I did. It was a big lopsided thing and it seemed to cast a shadow over all the other little rocks scattered about my feet.*

She continued, "Jesus is with you. He wants to help you pick it up." *I could barely look at Him. There was so much shame around this heavy load, and yet Jesus smiled at me as together we lifted it up about waist high.*

"Now, Jesus is going to help you throw it away. One, two, three!" *And with that, Jesus and I swung that big rock called "Odd" off the side of a cliff, where it smashed below in a million pieces against an enormous boulder named "Truth."*

By now I was weeping with relief; I had carried this burden since childhood—since not looking like or having common interests with my adoptive parents, since befriending the girls who were picked on in school instead of joining the popular girls, since being the uptight one among other theatre artists, and the eccentric one among conservative Christian ladies. It was the first time in months that I could actually feel my feelings and cry. My counselor, seeing an obvious breakthrough, wrapped up the visualization exercise by suggesting that Jesus was giving me something to remember this moment, something I could hold in my hand whenever I began to doubt that the burden of "Odd" was really gone for good. *Right then, I watched Jesus press a small green stone in my hand. It wasn't evenly shaped, and there were spots on it, but somehow it still attracted the eye. Jesus put His arm around my shoulders and looked deeply into my eyes with love. He told me that the little stone, like me, wasn't perfect, but it was unique and beautiful, and exactly how it was designed to be.*

When my counselor heard about the little rock, she suggested that I stop by a specialty shop in the nearby mall on the way home from my appointment. Something important had happened for me in that exercise, and she wanted me to find a rock keepsake, like the one Jesus had given me in the vision, to hold as a reminder of progress made in my recovery journey. I liked the idea, but honestly, I was much too excited to stop on the way home. This was the first time in months I began to feel like me. I couldn't wait to get home and see my family. When I arrived home, my older son (then about 14) greeted me right away. He could tell something was changed, happier, **better** with his mom. I asked him about his childhood polished rock collection and if I could borrow a rock for a while; in a flash he ran upstairs to retrieve it for me. "Mom, you can have all of 'em!"

"No, thank you, Honey, but if it's ok with you, maybe I'll keep one." I opened the little suede pouch and guess which was the very first stone to tumble out? Yup. It's small and green, uneven with spots on it. *It's not perfect, but it's unique and beautiful, and exactly the way it was designed to be.*

Life opens up in an entirely new way once you not only believe about the vastness of Jesus' love in your head, but actually receive it in your heart. See, Jesus knows you intimately. He knows what moves you and what makes you truly feel special. Through the years I have joyfully discovered the many ways He will reach into my day just to show me He's thinking of me. Some people call these wonderful little reminders "God Winks" or "God Kisses." What I have discovered is that the more you notice them, (*and thank Him for them*) the more you'll see!

I still remember the very first time I recognized that He was "kissing" me. I've always been a Fall Girl. I love the cooler fresh crisp air, wearing cozy sweaters and scarves, and seeing the beauty of colorful autumn leaves. Speaking of the leaves, way before I moved to a region in which the trees actually turned in the fall, I used a screensaver on my computer of an autumn scene that regularly captured my imagination. *One day I would experience natural beauty like that…*

Fast forward a few years and we were living in the Seattle area where in addition to the evergreens, there are a large number and variety of deciduous trees which turn all kinds of golden, orangey, red, and even purple hues each autumn. Gorgeous drives along tree-lined roads became a highlight for me each year, but in this particular year, once I knew the depths of God's love just for me, I started seeing things in a whole new way. It began simply: I was driving on the way to my house one day when a tree suddenly and inexplicably dropped about thirty leaves just in front of me as I passed underneath it. There was no wind, no rhyme or reason for it, EXCEPT, I had just begun learning about "God Kisses." *Could this be one?* I remember wondering about it and I decided to thank Jesus for the gift, when it happened again! In fact, it happened three more times before I made it to my driveway. Fluttering clouds of red and russet leaves, falling like confetti on a New Year's Day parade, suddenly floating down again and again as I drove by. This was NO COINCIDENCE! He was delighting in delighting me, and I was giggling and blushing like a school girl by the time I got home.

I will never forget that fall; Jesus thrilled me with the leaves throughout the season—on walks and on several more drives, and once when I was coaching my pastor friend. Dale, an associate pastor overseeing small groups, would make an appointment for help with his speaking delivery the two times a year when he was called upon to share a message at his church. On this occasion, as Dale stood with his back to my living room window, first 2 leaves floated down behind him, then 5 or 6 dropped, and soon more and more rained down as I worked really hard not to burst out loud with laughter! Looking back, it was a spectacular introduction to the world of "God Kisses" and to the wonder of becoming more fully alive to His presence.

Throughout the years Jesus has surprised me with "God Kisses" that were funny, ones that were instructive, some that supported me in times of loss, and ones that were romantic. *There is no mistaking that I am His Girl.* My most recent experience was two days ago at the local Chick Fil-A. I was in the drive-through nearing the dinner hour and the lines were very long. Chick Fil-A is one of my son's favorite go-to fast food meals, but as I am allergic to peanut oil, I am less familiar with the menu. Anyway, two helpful attendants were assisting customers in the two parallel lines that would eventually weave together into one around the corner of the building at the drive-through window. I was picking up dinner to take home and had my son's order written on a post-it note—down to the specific add-ons for the sandwich and what kind of soda he wanted—but for myself I just knew to order the grilled chicken sandwich. I didn't order a meal, I had water and soda at home. It wasn't until after I placed my order and snaked my way down along the side of the building that I first saw the actual posted menu sign. Instantly I was disappointed. I didn't know they had chocolate shakes! The more I thought about it, the more I wish I had ordered one. It had been a long day and I could really use a treat. I knew there was no ice cream in the house. I resigned myself to the fact that it was indeed too late to change my order; the restaurant was already so busy and the last thing I wanted to do was to frustrate a tired customer in one of the cars behind me. So I just smiled, putting the milkshake out of my mind as I paid the young man swiping credit cards. "It's my pleasure to serve you." As I approached the pick-up window I was distracted by a driver in a small truck, backing up from a parking space directly towards my car, and I sent up a quick arrow prayer "Help me, Lord!" that he wouldn't hit me as I waited in what was already a traffic snarl. Fortunately, with inches to spare he was able to turn and go while I waited my turn to move forward and pick up my order. Imagine my utter surprise when the restaurant worker approached my window with the bag, my son's soda and a chocolate milkshake! "Would you like a free chocolate milkshake? We made an extra." *Would I?!* Once again God decided to show me how He cares about the little things in my day. Joyfully I thanked Him all the way home.

Are you intimately aware of how much Jesus loves you? Yes, YOU alone. Are you experiencing a relationship with Him that makes your life full and rich and ALIVE right now, not just something you expect will happen when you get to heaven some day? If God hasn't turned everything upside down for you, giving you more Joy and Peace and Love and Freedom than you ever imagined possible, it's time to lean in and ask Him to show Himself, believing that He will!!

From the earliest days of our performance ministry, even before either of us had dealt with our own baggage or recognized "God Kisses" in our lives, my ministry partner and I discovered how God knew every woman's heart needs. Regardless of what material or what content was shared at each event, there would be women after the performances who would line up to speak with Tracie or me. Without any knowledge of our own personal histories, women would seek me out to share about their own issues with depression, concerns over a loved one with Alzheimer's, or raising a child on the spectrum. These were all things I could relate to, and in the sharing—in the knowledge that we're not alone—there was great comfort and blessing for each of us. Likewise, women with marital problems were drawn to Tracie like a magnet. Together they would talk and cry, hug and console one another with the loving arms of Jesus. See, God doesn't lump us all together and He knows there isn't a one-for-all-method to encourage His children. He designed us with different personalities, placed us in different environments with all different kinds of upbringings. He knows we have different ways of learning and we are moved by different kinds of experiences and forms of communication. Once we become Believers, we're given our own unique spiritual gifts or gift mix. Undoubtedly, our Heavenly Father will speak to you, or relate to you in very different ways than I'm sharing here. I'm hoping that that in itself brings tremendous comfort and proof of how he loves YOU. One of the most amazing things about His love was when I discovered that, unlike with broken human beings, I didn't have to compete for it, or compare my faith walk (usually poorly) against someone else's journey. Jesus IS Love. He can't love any one of us more or less than anyone else! The point is He Loves us, and He wants us all to know it. I have had the privilege of being asked to speak at several women's events over the last decade. Each and every time I have prayed earnestly to share only what He wants shared, and asked Him for input as I've crafted each talk. While there have been different topics, themes, or emphasis requested and delivered for different hosting organizations, one thing has remained the same. "Tell them I love them," He says into my spirit. "Tell them I LOVE them."

One of my favorite love stories happened two Christmases ago (December 2018). I was asked to speak for a women's brunch at a tiny new start-up church. Pastored by a woman who had become familiar with our performance ministry in a different church years before, this new home was established to come alongside addicts, former addicts, and the families who loved them. She recommended me to the new women's event planner and here, two years after our ministry formally closed its doors, I was thrilled to be invited to share in the day. I really had no idea what to expect. The church only had 16 regular attenders, including men, women, and 2 children. Yet, the event planner and the pastor believed that this was something they were called to do, and so they stepped out in faith, trusting God to bring the ladies. *More than 60 women showed up that day!*

They told me the theme was "Angels Among Us" and asked if in addition to my talk after lunch, I could perform a little monologue at the opening of the morning. I prepared a fun piece about a guardian angel and put together a costume complete with golden helmet, sword, and breastplate over a long white gown. When the ladies began to arrive, I stashed my regular clothes in the bathroom, and, fully dressed in angel garb, hid in the kitchen so as to surprise the women upon my entry. The event planner would give me a sound cue signaling when it was time to enter. However, once the morning got going and there was such an exciting number of attendees, the event planner forgot about me in the process of raffling prizes and playing games and the like. We had arranged that I would enter right after Christmas carols, but they had long since passed. So, I sent word to the pastor that I would change into my clothes and we'd skip the monologue and I would just speak at the brunch as planned. She promptly sent word back to stay put and she'd play my sound cue. I'm not sure who was more surprised, the ladies or me when, as I entered the room, instead of having the ladies seated at tables facing the front as expected, they were all on their feet around the perimeter of the room! Anyway, after a few awkward maneuvers and some exaggerated comedy, I charged back out of the room waving my sword as I escaped into the bathroom for my "quick change." Darting into the stall where my clothes had been set aside, I began stripping off the angel costume as I could hear the applause dying down and the event planner resume her game. Maybe 10 seconds went by and the bathroom door opened. I could hear a woman's footsteps, her quick gasp of air as the door closed behind her, and then she began to sob.

Now what do I do? I thought. I was standing in the stall in my underwear. *Should I come out and see if I could help? Should I talk to her through the door?* It occurred to me that maybe she needed a moment of privacy to collect herself so I just froze in position, hoping she wouldn't realize I was there. I didn't have to worry for long. The pastor had seen the woman's hasty retreat and came into the bathroom right away after her. "Are you ok?" the pastor asked.

"I don't know why I'm here," the woman cried. "I was driving down the road and my car turned up this driveway..." She went on through the tears to say that she had lost her job, her boyfriend left her, she had been staying on friends' couches, and the storage unit people were going to take her stuff and sell it if she didn't pay her bill by the next day. "I don't why I'm here," she repeated. "I don't belong in church... I just saw the cars and I said, Please God, I need an angel! And then I came in the lobby... and an angel ran right in front of me into the bathroom!"

His timing takes my breath away.

The pastor assured the woman 'why she was there,' introduced her to me, and then proceeded to invite the woman to sit at her table. By the end of the brunch, between the pastor, the event planner, and the women they had assembled at the event, the woman was sent away with a job, an appointment with a Christian counselor, potential housing, and a cashier's check for the storage unit. The Church behaved like the Church that day, and the woman saw Jesus in all His glory. That brunch will forever stand out to me as an example of God's love for each one of His children. While I know many of us were blessed that day, I think the entire event was designed with that one woman in mind.

Do you remember when you were the One? If you need any assurance, just ask Him; in His Love and Goodness, God literally pursues us all the days of our lives!

CHAPTER 2

Created for Purpose

So we are convinced that every detail of our lives
is woven together to fit into God's perfect plan
of bringing good into our lives, for we are His
lovers who have been called to fulfill His designed
purpose. (Rom 8:28 TPT)

I was in the check-out line at the grocery store today when it
happened again… "That's quite a brace. How's your knee doing?"
"Fine. I was in a car accident years ago. This just keeps it safe."
Sometimes they press further. "Did you tear your ACL?", "You
must have really wrecked it, huh?", or frequently they'll say, "It looks
painful; does it hurt?"

*The questions never offend me; in fact now I have a natural opening
to launch into my walking miracle story! Only time and audience
interest will tell if the person (people) on the other end will stay to hear
some or all of the little miracles that have unfolded around the main
story over the last 30+ years.*

When I was 19 and home for the summer after my first year
in college, I thought I was all that and a bag of chips. Having just

performed in a very successful three-woman show as a Freshman in a prestigious university with a well-known Theatre Arts program, I could see myself headed for Broadway in a few short years. That summer, in an instant—and over the weeks that followed—I humbly found out that "chips" can be smashed into smithereens. I was working full time at an office temp job, but that didn't keep me from joining my theatre friends for their cast party after the show, about 20 miles away from my house. It also didn't stop me from sampling the tequila puffs. *Throughout high school, I had a reputation among my theatre friends as more of a "goody-two shoes" bookworm than a true artist. I honestly believed that I was only accepted into this fun, loveable group of creative types by virtue of my acting abilities. Now, no longer even part of the group, I spent the summer trying to prove that I could be colorful and free-spirited too.* The party was still going strong at 2:30 in the morning when I decided I had had enough and headed for home. The last thing I remember was the glare of the headlights from the cars I passed as I headed down the busy 4-lane boulevard at about 35 mph. While to this day, I don't think I was actually drunk, I <u>was</u> really tired, and I fell asleep at the wheel. Fortunately, I didn't turn into the opposite facing traffic and hurt anyone else with my stupidity. Unfortunately, instead, in my mom's little Honda Civic, I crashed headfirst into a telephone pole.

Some of the miraculous details came to be known early on: The collision literally tore my right knee in half, with the exception of the main artery (so I didn't bleed out), and the main nerve (so I wasn't paralyzed). My doctor told me it was the worst thing he had ever seen that didn't have to be amputated. Looking back today from the perspective of a woman with two adult children, I can only imagine what my mom went through. First there was the late night/early morning phone call from the highway patrol: "Your daughter's been in an accident. She's not badly hurt but we're taking her to the hospital for some tests. What do you want us to do with the car?" Then there would be the year of worry...

I was told I wouldn't be able to go back to school on time. I did. I was told I may never walk again. I did. With all glory to God (although at the time I just knew there was a supernatural "Force" looking out after me), I recovered much better than anyone expected. My surgeon had heard of a new post-operative therapy to minimize scar tissue, and so I had teams of doctors visiting my hospital room each day to watch the rented Continuous Passive Motion Machine (commonly sent home with knee replacement patients today.) Upon returning to school, and though I wasn't a student athlete, I was given special permission to use the university's Sports Rehab Facility at peak hours and at no cost! The referring specialist said my injuries were so bad, the physical therapists on staff could learn something from working with me.

My Sophomore year is somewhat of a blur. I committed faithfully to the physical therapy, and believing Broadway might now be off the table, I decided to add education courses and a teaching credential to my course load. *It amazes me that I might not otherwise have ever discovered the passion I have for teaching and coaching others.* By Thanksgiving I was off the crutches, by April I was half-running and half-climbing down the scaffolding as Shakespeare's "Juliet" in an acting class exercise, and by the year's end I was only required to wear my brace for jumping, running, and any exercise that would put stress on my knees. I walked without a limp and for many years, unless you looked for it, you would never know that anything like that had happened to me. *Talk about a miracle!*

Sometimes when I talk about my accident to Christians, they will ask me if I think God was punishing me that summer. If this is your thought, let me assure you, our Heavenly Father isn't a wrathful angry capricious God up on High who enjoys inflicting pain and suffering on mankind. We are His beloved children—every one of us![lvii]

God allowed the accident to happen for my own good, and today I look upon it as one of His greatest gifts to me. Spending two weeks in a hospital—where initially I had to rely on the kindness of nurses for basic hygiene care, where I became uncomfortably aware of how my own poor choices could not only ruin my future, but cause great distress to others, and where I realized life itself was a beautiful and fragile thing—changed my entire outlook. My thinking and attitudes which had become very me-centered in college now returned to an others' perspective. In the blink of an eye this near tragic event taught me humility, empathy, and gratitude in ways I might not have developed had the accident not occurred. It taught me to value the little things, and to finally grasp in a real way that something much bigger than humankind was at work in our lives!

Yet, as I was to learn, the immediate aftermath was only a part of the story.[viii]

In the late 80's we became aware of a modern-day plague that had spread around the world. By that point we now understood how AIDS was contracted, and we discovered with horror its long incubation, and that someone could have been infected a decade earlier without showing any symptoms. At the time, receiving a positive HIV test was akin to a death sentence. I lost dear friends and beloved teachers to this hideous wasting disease, and I'll never forget that hopeless grief I felt at bedside visits and funerals before I knew the peace of heaven.

By early 1989 this became even more personal. News stories began to earnestly recommend that anyone and everyone who fell into a high-risk group should be tested. That was me! I survived the car accident—**in the San Francisco Bay Area, in July of 1983**—after receiving 5 pints of blood in transfusion, from potentially 5 different donors. Blood banks weren't screened for AIDS until 1984. Tim and I were engaged at this point and when I decided to get tested, we spent a lot of time thinking optimistically, but considering the worse-case scenario. *Would he still want to marry me if I tested positive for HIV? Would we be able to have children? Would I lose my job? (At the time I was working for a large HMO in Southern California, touring in "Professor Bodywise", a professional children's*

26

theatre show on health and safety.) This is when "in sickness and in health" really hits home. The 10-day waiting period for the blood test results crawled by, but again, God had other plans for me, and I was spared once more.

Through the years, since I've become a Christ Follower, I've had many opportunities to share about my miraculous healing with many others, in both formal (ministry) and informal settings. *Don't you love how He can use our messes for blessings?* I can tell as their eyes widen that they too are amazed at God's goodness! The story of how I went back to a surgeon 20 years after the accident never ceases to drop jaws... By then, nearing 40, my knee began to get tired or stiff after long walks with the dog, or following performances. I was also having some trouble with my IT band and when I went to an orthopedic specialist, he warned me to expect the worst. Reviewing my original diagnosis and discharge papers, he ordered an x-ray while we discussed the possibilities of surgery, and medications for the arthritis that most certainly must be riddling my joint. Imagine his surprise and my delight when the x-ray showed no extra damage beyond the original injury! There was no build-up of arthritis, and no cause for surgery! The doctor came to me half smiling and half shaking his head. According to the general consensus, apparently the procedure used in my original surgeries following the accident "never worked." Considered experimental, this procedure was abandoned shortly after it was first tested! *Another astonishing fact for those who struggle with faith and need some kind of proof when faced with an encounter with Jesus—to God alone be all the glory for my miraculous healing!*

Still, my favorite story in the aftermath of the accident isn't about me at all. In 2011 my brother called me out of the blue. While I was thrilled because I hadn't heard from him during the previous four years, I was also really surprised and curious. He was really agitated and he urged me to get in touch with my original orthopedic surgeon to track down the name of one of his former nurses.

Filling me in on a part of the story of my accident I had never heard before, my brother told me about the woman he had picked up in a bar that night. He was 21 at the time with a lot of baggage of his own, and you and I can well imagine what he was thinking when he decided to take her home with him (*to our mother's house*) after the bar closed. You might also be able to picture her; according to Kurt she was a petite brunette who looked "rode hard and put up wet." When the two of them arrived at my mother's house in the middle of the night, Mom was awake and nearly hysterical. She had just received the phone call from the police advising her of my accident. My brother and this woman headed out for the hospital, where she insisted that he take a different route than the faster, back way as he had planned. Now, instead, driving down the main boulevard, they came across the accident scene still in progress; the paramedics were using the jaws of life to pry open the car and pull me out. My brother and the woman followed the ambulance to the hospital where she immediately talked her way into the emergency room trauma center. **Explaining to the ER team that she was a former orthopedic nurse, she convinced the doctors considering amputation to hold off on the procedure, so that she could call my brilliant surgeon, asking him to take my case!** *Miracle- right? For nearly 30 years I thought my surgeon "happened" to be on call that night.* In the whirlwind of activity that followed, this unlikely angel disappeared without a trace.

At my brother's urging, I tried to find out about this woman, but with nothing but a vague 28- year-old physical description and a phone number that reached a doctor's exchange (my surgeon had since retired), I struck out. When I called my brother back a few days later, he told me why he had been so persistent earlier. Now living in a small town in Kansas, he had experienced a very strange visitor. One night, he came home late from work and, not wanting to disturb his sleeping girlfriend, he decided to crash on the couch. Later, when he himself was in a deep sleep, a woman walked through the unlocked front door, made her way to the bedroom without waking him, and sat on the edge of the bed. My brother's girlfriend later described the woman as a petite brunette who looked "rode hard and put up wet." The stranger asked my brother's girlfriend about "Cara's knee," made a little more small talk to the bewildered girlfriend, and then quietly stood up and walked out the door! My brother's girlfriend—who had no idea he even had a sister—woke him immediately with the story, and wouldn't you know, that would be enough for him to re-connect with me? *In my family this in itself is a miracle; we have lots of estranged relatives. However, now, even more extraordinarily, my brother was interested in talking about the possibility of God's existence! To this day, Kurt refers to this unusual visitor as his angel.*

When we talk about God's healing, most people will immediately think of the physical realm. Some can testify to the stories of people throwing down their crutches in a revival service, or stumping doctors when inoperable cancerous tumors suddenly disappear. I too can stand before anybody today and declare unequivocally, God is still in the healing business. Yet, I'm convinced the health of our physical bodies is secondary. Jesus wants our thoughts, our emotions, our relationships, indeed our very LIVES transformed and made FULL. It is from this place of wholeness that our testimonies can powerfully point to the truth of the gospel message.

In fact, I learned early on in my faith walk that God would use both my new physical reality and the now redeemed, messiest parts of my old life to become the very catalyst that would propel me into ministry. I have a heart for the shame-filled, *unworthy of love* women in no small part because I was one of them! I also discovered that the skills and passions I had already developed early in life for performance weren't a mistake or a silly waste of time by a naive young woman like me. When used for His purposes, God infuses your abilities supernaturally.

A few months after I asked Jesus to be my Savior I was cast in my first role in a church production. *Unlike worship ministry, drama ministry has a history of alternately being embraced and then discarded by the church. Thankfully drama ministry was "in" during this new awakening for me! It allowed me to serve and grow from my strengths immediately.*

For some quick background context: I performed in many productions over the years, both amateur and professional. In the beginning theatre was an escape for me, and later it became so much more. I had always loved the process of rehearsing for a show, the teamwork, and the thrill of watching something truly touching grow from simple words on a page. There was a life to it, albeit an artificial one. But for a young woman without a solid sense of identity and the fear that she didn't measure up to others, there was great comfort in being able to try on the lives of different characters in situations completely unlike my own. For me, it was always about the work and the joy; I never had a goal of becoming famous as some of my classmates and castmates did. A good drama, like any good story, can teach and inspire, entertain and provoke, illustrating something about life that wouldn't be recognized in any other medium. Every performance of a live production has its own existence—distinctly created by the actors each night and impacted by each individual audience. **Yet with church ministry, it was as though a whole new world opened up and for the first time, I understood what live theatre could be according to the Creator.** After these shows, instead of complimenting me on my performance, audience members would say, "You blessed me" or, *and this still brings tears to my eyes,* "I could see Jesus through you." Wow.

Still a new Believer but eager to pour myself into my church family with everything I had, I taught drama in church settings, I wrote and directed productions for children's ministry, and I performed in shows as I could. Once we moved to the Seattle area, auditioning for the Christmas musical seemed like a great way to connect with this new church family. However Jesus, the One who came to give us more than we expect or imagine, had bigger plans in mind...

Late in the fall of 2001 at around 3 o'clock in the morning, while still in the rehearsal process for a church Christmas production, The Voice woke me again. "Get up." *To answer your questions—1) No, I didn't actually hear God's Voice out loud through my ears; but I did truly hear it audibly in my spirit. 2) No, I don't hear His Voice regularly; this was the second, and so far, the last time I have heard from Him in this way.* **God can choose any way He wants to get our attention.**

I got out of bed immediately, excitedly rushing into the living room where I could write. I can only describe it as a massive download: No longer audible, but nevertheless streaming through my consciousness, God was giving me a mission in full detail! I took pages of copious notes, furiously trying to keep up with the inspiration as He revealed a very original ministry. Somehow it would combine performance and heartfelt testimony, acting and music, things that would bring laughter and encouragement and perhaps some tears too. It would tour, not just inside churches, but outside too, where people are really looking for hope. And God would give me a partner– a wonderfully talented, wears-her-heart-on-her-sleeve, deeply committed Believer, whom I had just met and was working with in our church's upcoming Christmas play. I waited until maybe 6:30 am to call Tracie, figuring that, as another mom with young children, she'd be awake by then.

"Tracie! God woke me up and we're supposed to start a ministry, kind of like a variety show, and we'll…" (Honestly, I don't remember exactly what I said but I know I was excited and I just blurted out this fantastic idea—way before either one of us had had her morning coffee!) I do remember though, Tracie's response– "What??!!!" God had called her earlier and told her that she was going to be touring and performing. For a few months, Tracie had been trying to figure out what to do with this information!

Another confirmation occurred a couple of days later. Tracie and I were at a rehearsal and talking things over during a break when a third woman from the cast ran over to us, sharing that God had told her the three of us were going to be working on some kind of touring, performance and speaking ministry! *It was really wild!* The three of us agreed to pray about it individually through the rest of the Christmas season, and then to get together to start seriously planning this right after the new year. By the time we met again, we were ON FIRE, completely convinced that this new ministry would really happen. We had a lot of important things in common, and the different ideas that came out would be important for shaping our mission goals and policies. It was such an exciting time of give and take, but we also were very clear on the One who was giving us this opportunity.

In that very first meeting we also talked honestly about things in our life to be covered in prayer—things that the enemy could use to render us ineffective. Then, before we ended our time together, we began tossing around ideas for a name for our group. We wanted it to be memorable, unique, rooted in faith, and yet NOT something that would instantly block us from secular events. As it turned out, the three of us all related to the same Bible story. *There are no coincidences, remember?* Like the woman at the well in the story from John 4, we all had some brokenness regarding past relationships; like her we had all looked for love in the wrong places; like her we all knew life was different/BETTER with Jesus in it!! A few days later, with some web research and more prayer, "Drawing Water" was born.

There was an immediate early blossoming of our ministry as our Heavenly Father equipped us for this new adventure. But there were also birth pangs, especially after our third member decided to remove herself from our performing team. *Growth and expansion are funny things… sometimes there are quick spurts with a lot of exciting changes, sometimes things seem to plateau for a while with nothing much happening as a new normal is established and practiced.*

While our ministry developed and grew over the next 14 years, my walk with the Lord also deepened and expanded. I'll be bringing up different things I learned during my Drawing Water years throughout this book, how could I not? However, for the purposes of this chapter, I want to focus on a real-life example of what it means when Believers learn that God will empower (or equip) those He has called. In our case, we were a couple of actors, what did we know about running a non-profit ministry? And yet through the Lord's extraordinary orchestration of all the pieces, we had everything we needed to play the music!

The What: When our ministry started we had a vision for the light-hearted nature of our performances but quickly discovered there was a huge gap between the content material we hoped to find, and what was actually out there. Good clean wholesome material is hard to come by in our world, and things described as Christian plays or sketches were so cheesy. Add to that the concern of having to pay for royalties when we ourselves would be on a ministry shoestring budget, can you see how this ministry vision could have sunk before it even sailed? The funny thing is, I don't think we ever actually worried about it at all. From the time the three of us started meeting, God, in His gracious faithfulness, inspired my writing. Now I'm not saying all of my pieces were successful; in the beginning, especially, there were a number of this-will-have-to-do scenes or monologues included to round out our program. Yet so many truly just flowed out from the Spirit—pieces that underscored a knowledge far beyond what I yet possessed. Some were poignant sketches that were both loving and truth-filled; some were delightfully silly scenes that helped our audiences remember them years later. Eventually, Tracie began writing a few of our sketches as well, but trust me, we both knew when something really hit home—encouraging wounded hearts or bringing up great belly laughs—Jesus was our master playwright.

The Where: Before we began formulating what we would do or how we would do it, we met with our church's drama team leader to inform him that while we still planned to participate in the church drama program as we were able, we were being called into our own touring ministry. He looked at us with the funniest expression on his face. He had just been contacted to put together a dinner theatre event for a large Christian organization's fundraising evening and he knew this wasn't something he could do. Would we like the opportunity to provide the entertainment? *Amazing, right?! It gets better…*

In our first year, following a short performance at a Christian Worship Arts event, we were approached by a woman who asked if we could write something for, and perform at, a luncheon for her new ministry group for single women. Although there were maybe 20 women in her group, her close friend who "happened to be" the Women's Director of CRISTA, (a large Christian organization in Seattle that had many ministry branches) was also there for support. This friend caught the vision that God had given us, and invited us to share at CRISTA's upcoming Christian Women's Ministry Fair. Our participation that first year, and by the word of mouth that spread following it, launched Drawing Water into a touring schedule!

The Who: When we needed guest actors to play husbands for the large dinner theatre event, though we had no ministry track record, no video or evidence of what was to come, barely anything scripted, and the knowledge that we wouldn't be able to pay them adequately for their time or service, God provided two Spirit-filled, talented guys to volunteer with our little experiment. He also fanned the flames of an incredible group of men and women who would come alongside as our Board of Directors. How they were drawn to a funny little out-of-the-box performance ministry steered by a couple of actresses blows my mind to this day! And wouldn't you know, though the Board went through changes with different Directors through the years, the Lord made sure we always had at least one pastor sitting on it for accountability. Whatever the need, God supplied our human resources—musicians, web designers, tech crews for special events, guest actors, a support team when we traveled to prisons and women's shelters, and even a tax preparer who was familiar with non-profits and independent contractors.

The How: *You're going to love this one!* From the beginning we were very blessed to know one of the pre-eminent touring dramatic artist ministers of the time, David Shelton. With a heart for Jesus and a recognition that as two women, we filled a unique niche, David graciously shared wisdom and specific strategies from a life on the road in Christian ministry. His wife Deborah, who acted as his extraordinary business manager also befriended us, and later even served on our Board. She taught us how to make contracts that protected us, as well as providing services for various hosting organizations. She also shared about becoming registered with the state and about the importance of becoming a recognized 501 (c) 3 non-profit. *In a world looking to mock and put out of commission anything having to do with Jesus, a Christian organization needs to be SO careful about ensuring everything is done according to the laws of the land.*

We knew the legal paperwork for the non-profit status could take a year or more to be approved for a small outfit like ours. I did some research, bought a how-to book and diligently began working on the project. Then, *and this tickles me to this day*, when I mentioned it in an email to college friends as we shared updates from our lives for the 20th reunion, I "happened" to hear back from one of my classmates who now worked for a law firm. You guessed it—not only did they do this kind of legal work, but her firm was offering to check over our paperwork, pro bono! There was no mistaking God's hand all over this; we had our Federal approval and status within four months of our application.

Is there something God has placed on <u>your</u> heart to begin doing? Something that you have put off because you don't think you have the resources, the skills, or the knowledge to accomplish it on your own? Don't let fear stop you in your tracks! Maybe you're wondering if God REALLY called you, or if this is just your desire getting carried away? **Start stepping out in faith.**

One sure way of knowing that you are following God's calling on your life is if things start falling into place in ways you never could have planned or imagined.

One more thing I wanted to mention while I'm talking about the Lord's divine plans for your life and His healing of whatever physical or emotional baggage that may have kept you from your true calling. When you trust Him, He can use all of your pain for good. From the midst of your mess, your faith can inspire others. Remember that our purpose isn't necessarily the same thing as our ministry. As I've learned through the years, though my ministry has changed—sometimes there's a platform and audience involved, sometimes there's a challenge in my family, sometimes it's somebody seated next to me on an airplane—my God-given purpose continues to pour out of a heart that's eternally grateful. Once we come to know Jesus, once we experience the abundance of the LIFE we are meant to live, we are driven to share the awe and the love, the peace and our total joy of this relationship with others.

We have become (God's) poetry... Even before we were born, God planned in advance our destiny and the good works we would do to fulfill it! Eph 2:10 (TPT)

CHAPTER 3

An Education on Discernment

Be self-controlled and alert. Your enemy the devil prowls around like a roaring lion looking for someone to devour. (1 Peter 5:8 NIV)

I started having the dreams early in my walk with Jesus; God wanted me to know that there was a very REAL enemy on the prowl and for me to learn to recognize the presence of evil. He knew that I would have to be prepared for the opposition that would come against my ministry and against me personally. He knew that having grown up in a dysfunctional home environment with no boundaries, I would need extra reinforcement in this area. In the same spirit, I'm going to share a few of these dreams here with you, not to stir up fear, but to help you see as I did, the importance of learning what is of God and what is not.

In the first dream, a group of hikers were with me as together we suddenly came to a large opening on the trail. What had been a fairly narrow mountain path shielded on either side with towering trees gave way to a small adjacent meadow of flowers, and beyond them, the gaping mouth of a cave. One of the men in the group took off through the flowers heading for the rock face to enter the cave, but I knew something was very wrong. The flowers were beautiful and exotic looking, but they were too perfect, almost waxy, and I sensed the danger building in my Spirit. I called out to the man to come back to the trail with the group, but ignoring me, he ran ahead and scrambled up the side of the rock face for what seemed like 5 or 6 feet to the cave opening. "Come back! Don't go in the cave!" I called, but still he climbed until he managed to hoist himself up into the mouth of the cave. Standing triumphantly, he turned to wave at us, but it wouldn't be for long. Suddenly, the flowers changed and began moving. Turning into many tentacles of a creeping vine, the flowers crept up the side of the rock face and into the cave, where they both held the man and climbed over him, swallowing him up whole, and he was gone.

In another dream I was in a large open-air stadium waiting for the big event—there was to be a total eclipse of the sun and everyone had gathered to see it. There were others with me as we watched from high up in the stands, but a great crowd was below on the field. They were partying and carrying on with their own activities and I noticed that none of them were even looking to the skies. Then the sky went black as night and the stadium lights turned on. I could see the people on the field, still laughing and drinking and so completely consumed with whatever they were doing, they didn't even notice the eclipse. "Look up!" I shouted down to them, but no one heard me. That's when from somewhere behind the darkened sun, four rocket missiles suddenly appeared, heading straight for us. "Look out!" I called down once more to the people partying on the field, but no one even looked up. Watching from high above in the stands we could see explosions and fire down below… and then I woke up.

Dreams that impress me as being from God are memorable, highly detailed, things that I've never thought about in my waking hours, and Biblically sound. In the first dream for example, trust me when I tell you, I'm not a hiker; the last place you would find me is leading a group up a mountain trail. To me it immediately brought to mind to watch out for enticing traps, choosing to stay on the narrow path *(what looks good and seems good isn't always good.)* The second one seemed more connected to end times events. *(The sun went dark, and "as in the days of Noah," the people were partying and carrying on, oblivious to the signs around them.)* Also, significantly, while both of these dreams contained images of evil, I didn't wake up feeling afraid or defeated by them. Instead they left me feeling MORE certain of our Father's love.

In these kinds of early God-given dreams I was usually cast in the role of witness, a Jeremiah type of prophet. I could see the darkness and I called out the danger to people I knew were heading into trouble, but sadly, they ignored my warnings. Later in my spiritual discernment training, I would have to face evil directly.

Once I dreamed that I had to cross a street, the other side of which was in enemy territory. There was a barrier and a guard in full military gear right in the middle of the road, and I knew that just going there would be risky. I noticed many people on an escalator that ascended up from my side of the street nearby. Taking the escalator meant they could avoid the trouble in the road by acting as witnesses as they watched the action from above. I remember thinking that normally I would be with them, but this time, I was being called into battle. I looked down and saw that I was wearing combat boots! Carrying two large packages in plain brown wrappers, I warily approached the security guard posted at the barrier in the center of the road. His eyes were dark and piercing as he stared at me, but he made no movement to stop me as I headed toward the barrier. There was no gate or pass through in the low wall at this area of the road, and I slowed to consider how I would manage the two packages as I climbed over it. Just then the guard from his post on the opposite side of the barrier, offered to help me with the boxes. I smiled and nodded quickly as I handed him the larger one, but immediately discovered my mistake. The second he took the package from my hands he turned and threw it onto the sidewalk behind him where it landed with a loud thud. He motioned for me to hand him the second package, but I held on to it firmly. This one was precious! I couldn't let him take it. I remember holding it close to my chest as I awkwardly maneuvered my body up and over the low wall. Relieved but now on high alert within the watchful eyes of the enemy, I moved quickly to gather up my other package on the far sidewalk. *I remember awakening to the idea that I would have to do my part to protect the priceless gifts given me by the Holy Spirit.*

A quick note on dreaming, as it can be quite controversial. There are many Christians in the prophetic community who are vastly more experienced than I am in this department. Some have even written books to help other believers interpret their dreams. I can only share with authority from my limited experience, but again, in writing this book, The Holy Spirit made it clear that this is an important chapter to include, just as it was important for me in my early growth. So here's what I know: God's Word tells us that Joseph, Daniel, John, and Peter all experienced some form of God-given dreams or visions, AND that God IS, WAS, and ALWAYS WILL BE the same. Furthermore, God's Word indicates that more and more of you will dream dreams and see visions as we grow closer to the final days before Jesus returns.[ix] One key is to learn to identify the source of the dreams. God isn't the only one who may attempt to catch our attention when we finally slow down after a busy day.

Imagine a dream in which you're running late, or not prepared for something at work. These are soulish/ fleshly dreams that come out of our own imaginations. *(I literally used to have the classic actor's nightmare—showing up on stage in the wrong play, not knowing my lines, or unable to find my costume.)* Often these kinds of dreams will appear in a season in which you're under stress—learning a new job, leaving a job, or even having challenges in a relationship. Sometimes these dreams will keep you up at night, but they don't tend to stick with you once you're fully awake and going through your day.

The enemy can also try to infiltrate your thoughts in the night hours. The demonic intention is to get you to be fearful, to doubt God's love, to doubt your salvation or worthiness, and to cause division. These dreams which contain sinful behaviors and desires can also negatively affect your peace after waking from them. So let me emphasize now, if this is going on for you, you must stop him in his oily tracks immediately! **You are a beloved child of God**. Ask the Holy Spirit to guard your heart and mind during your sleep, and keep vigilant. Sometimes dreams get hijacked midway through. A big part of my training has been to learn to cast my troubling thoughts on to Jesus (including those that come in dream form) before they get a toehold, and to be able to stand firm in my true identity when it comes under attack.

Once I was sufficiently able to do this, my education on discernment expanded and the Lord began to show me the presence of evil in the physical world around me. Again, I am no expert. There are those who are far more experienced as seers in the spiritual realm. If you suspect this may be your gift, there is a good book on the subject, The Veil by Blake Healy[x]. Vetted by Bill Johnson of Bethel Church, I would recommend it for a better understanding of the angelic and the demonic around us. I would suspect however, that this kind of discernment is a rare gift. Even when it comes to what little I've seen, some of you will find this bizarre and not a little unsettling. Let me reiterate, this in no way is meant to stir up fear. God never leaves us or forsakes us. For me, this was simply a time of training and testing. The best way I can describe these visual experiences is for you to imagine a thin, transparent overlay of spiritual truth on top of what was seen in the natural realm. Somehow, God would highlight things about the people around me in such a way, that I suddenly knew they were either practicing evil, or under its influence.

The first time I saw it, I was in the airport in Las Vegas on my way home. There was a young man, another traveling passenger who brought no carry-on bag whatsoever, and there was this very dark, death-like shadow over him. I spotted him immediately after going through security, and I knew that he was watching me intently. He followed me onto the automated transit system and as much as I was on high alert, it struck me that he was acting even more wary of me. When we separated and went to different gates, I regretted that I didn't say or do anything that might have helped him. I began wishing I had handed him my Bible from my tote bag, and I even circled the area of all the gates near mine in case I came upon him again. I didn't find him, but by then I had more peace after this weird encounter. Maybe God didn't want me to interact with this shadowy stranger after all? Maybe I was just supposed to learn and observe.

I've seen evil several times since then, especially while living in the Seattle area. I'm not talking about a fictional book and movie series about teenaged vampires from Forks, WA. There really are practicing witches in the Pacific Northwest. Once, Jesus pointed out the office manager at our former vet clinic. She wore a smock with little animals on it and one day, in the spiritual overlay, their eyes began to glow. It was then that I noticed from across the room, the pentagram ring she wore on her marriage finger, and that her nails—neatly trimmed in the natural—had changed in appearance to look more like claws. Another time it was evening and I pulled behind another car at a stoplight. On a regular stop I wouldn't have looked twice. But God highlighted a couple of tell-tale stickers that night that stood out among the dozen or so attached to the car's rear bumper ("My other car is a broomstick", "Put a spell on it.") He also showed me two women inside who were clearly laughing and pointing at something down the street. In my spirit I realized they were cursing something or someone and I began praying for the businesses, the lives, and the relationships of all in their circle of influence during the rest of my drive home. While God hasn't asked me to confront evil in any way, I am always led to pray for those who are trapped under it, or choosing to partner with it.

By now you might be wondering if evil is present around you too, and if so, would you recognize it in the spirit realm or while you're dreaming? We live in a broken world. In a year of a global pandemic, civil unrest and violence across America, fires, smoke, hurricanes and floods, and an economy that is threatening to leave more and more people behind and homeless, **you already know that evil is everywhere.** Yet, like me, you can not only recognize the darkness, you can stop it from entangling you in fear. How? By becoming grounded in the knowledge of God's character.

Start by getting into God's Word; learn about His promises. He is Faithful and True and will not go against His Word. If you can join a Bible study group, do it! If you only have time for a daily devotional, do that. Tune in to teaching on Christian broadcasts, find a Christian accountability partner, attend services either live or online where there is solid Biblical teaching. Then, in addition to the things you can come to know about the Lord, take time to get to know Jesus personally. Talk to Him, pour out your heart, spend time thanking Him for the little things (such as the God Kisses I've already mentioned). Knowing God's character is the only way to ensure that you won't get swayed by a dream, or turned around by false teaching.

Speaking of getting to know God's character, let's take a moment here for a quick reflection—There is one God in three persons. Throughout scripture we see evidence of how the Father, Son, and Holy Spirit work together in perfect unity. Sometimes however, because of poor teaching/theology, or because of some brokenness in our human relationships, people will have trouble relating to one or more of these three persons of God. God the Father is not out to punish you; Jesus is not just your buddy; the Holy Spirit isn't trying to manipulate you or spoil your fun. If you have any obstacles to experiencing intimacy with any of the three persons, I encourage you to begin speaking to Him immediately and often. He is waiting for you!

Today, I regularly talk to Abba (my Daddy), I spend time seeking the Spirit's wise counsel, and I am frequently overwhelmed with awe and joy by Jesus' loving presence.

I came so they can have real and eternal life, more and better life than they ever dreamed of. (John 10:10 MSG)

Would it surprise you to know that Jesus is funny? Whether it's over an amusing incident that He brings back to recall, or something new He stages to surprise and delight me during the day, Jesus gets my sense of humor and we love to laugh together! I have also been honored to be invited to join Him in mourning. I can't say that it has been easy to weep with Him over the lost and hurting. Yet I have grown closer to Him as I have come to understand at the deepest level His utter grief over our self-destructive choices and their painful consequences. This is not an uncaring distant deity; there is nothing impersonal about Him!

This story is about the first time Jesus asked me to mourn with Him over broken humanity.

We had a Drawing Water performance in a women's shelter in Monroe WA and though we had been there for their ladies on several other occasions, this time would remain with me. Usually the performances were held downstairs in the basement, where though the ceiling was low and we had to be careful not to hit it during our cheerleading routine, there was more space there to hold both our performance area and an audience area for the women to sit. This time however, one of their residents was in a wheelchair, and wanting everyone to be able to see our ministry offering, the house leaders asked us if we could reduce our space requirement and stuff everyone in the living room. We agreed and they had removed the sofas before we got there, replacing them with folding chairs, and Tracie and I minimized our movement to fit into an area that was roughly 5 ft across by 3' deep, and doing without our usual curtain, we simply turned our backs to the ladies to suggest entrances and exits, and for changing costume accessories.

To say we were on top of the audience is an understatement, but I remember it being one of those high energy shows where you could feel the Holy Spirit at work. The women were with us from the onset—laughing loudly, crying in recognition, hanging on to every message of hope. While there was a lot of fuss over the woman in the wheelchair, my eyes were drawn over and over to a woman who sat behind her and off to the left side of the audience. No one else paid any attention to this resident, but I could literally see her pain. In the Spirit overlay Her face looked to me as if it had been pinched off into four corners, two on either side of her forehead, and two on either side of her lower jaw. Her eyes were pulled into horizontal slits, and her lips were pursed so tightly that her mouth nearly disappeared. Throughout the program I would look over at her and though she always looked fiercely attentive, I never caught her smiling or wiping away a tear as the other women did. It was like she was frozen with that pointy face.

After the performance, the women near the woman in the wheelchair crowded around their friend, laughing and animated, and my partner Tracie joined them. I sat next to the pointy face woman asking how she was, and she immediately dissolved into tears. She talked about a terribly abusive childhood… repeatedly being locked in a closet… raped by her stepfather and two stepbrothers… disbelieved and unsupported by her mother. She talked of difficulties later… keeping a job… making friends… trusting anyone. When she was attacked and raped once more by someone she worked with, she believed the lie that somehow she had brought this on herself. That's when she decided to get a double mastectomy so that no one would want to touch her again. She talked and cried, I listened and held her hand. "Where was Jesus then?" she wanted to know. "Why wasn't He with me?"

I don't remember how I answered her or what I said, but I do remember I had a sudden vision of Jesus holding her as a little girl in that closet. I remember the Spirit directing me to share the things I was seeing with her, and to pray out loud over her. And I remember that by the end of our conversation, the woman's hard pointy edges were gone. When we said goodbye she now had a lovely soft oval face, beautiful ice blue eyes, and a peaceful smile. Little did I know that for me, this would be just the beginning of our encounter.

I sobbed during the entire hourlong drive home, and then I cried until I fell asleep that night. I cried off and on daily for nearly 2 ½ weeks, and the whole time I was intimately aware that Jesus was crying with me. We cried for this woman and so many like her. We cried over His precious children—about abuses that are inflicted on one another. We cried about rape and incest and self-mutilation. We cried until there were no more tears and the skin under my eyes and nose was raw and chapped.

While I now know there are people gifted with mercy and intercessory prayer who do this regularly, in the years since my first experience, I have been invited to weep with Jesus for only a few, very specific occasions. Perhaps because of my history with depression, He knows how much sadness I can handle before I internalize it. Perhaps He just wanted me to be familiar with this gift so that I might encourage other women I meet who have it but haven't yet received wisdom about it. Regardless, I now know His heart deeply, and I know how much pain He feels over our brokenness, and the eternally lost.

Two occasions where Jesus and I wept together in grief do stand out however, and I believe I am called to be a witness to them here. In the beginning of 2018 Abba let me know that for me, this would be a year of learning about His Glory. (I'll be talking about this in a later chapter but for now I'll just focus on the first month.) You see, before I would be ready to experience the Glory of His Presence, I had to first recognize how far humankind has fallen short of it. Jesus tenderly reminded me of His great love for me for a few days in preparation, but then I spent nearly 4 weeks in the depths of despair, repenting over all of the terrible things mankind has done. Again, Jesus wept with me, and again it was brutal. Sin is NEVER to be glossed over or compromised with, as many in today's church tend to do. Our sin, humanity's deliberate choices to walk away from God's ways, has caused so much of the pain and suffering we see today. If you want to know where Autism, Alzheimer's, Homosexuality, Gender Confusion, Mental Illness, Cancer and Addiction came from, just look to fallen man. I saw that over millennia, the sin which began with our earliest ancestors in the Garden of Eden literally corrupted our own gene pool.

Likewise, as I discovered with gut wrenching sobs for a few weeks in 2019, once we Americans began tolerating—and then practically welcoming—abortion, we gave free reign to Death and unleashed Suicide from the pit of hell. My younger son's best friend, a Believer who was tormented by gender confusion, took his own life just before his 23rd birthday. I hope you can hear my heart and the depths of Jesus' mourning over all of this. This has nothing to do with pointing fingers and political agendas. This is about returning to God's ways because He knows what's best for us! Talking about sin and repentance certainly isn't popular, but in these times, there couldn't be a more important urgent message. Too many church leaders either avoid the subject in our P.C. culture, or err the other way by brandishing judgment as a weapon while withholding grace.

If something here is stirring in you—maybe you've been arguing with another Christian about their beliefs, or maybe you're wondering if a long held belief of yours is actually grieving the Lord—please take your confusion to Jesus and spend some time reflecting on His Word. We will all have plenty of battles to fight in this lifetime, but it's important that we learn to fight on the same side against our real enemy. *Speaking of battles, one other kind of discernment that I have learned a lot about over the years has to do with recognizing opposition, especially that which attacks ministries, growing faith, and our very identity as Gods' children. Because this is such a common and a critical issue for all of us, I will be addressing this separately in Chapter 7, "Battle Ready."*

To wrap up this rather intense chapter, however, I wanted to focus on something uplifting Jesus has shown me. A couple of years ago I was working in a high-end spa in the Seattle area, and one of my occasional duties was to put the battery operated candles in the candle holders in the lounge and in each of the providers' rooms before the spa opened. I always enjoyed the quiet before the day got started. It tickled me to be bringing light into the darkness, (true on multiple levels in this environment) and I regularly prayed prayers of healing and protection and blessing over each space. One day as I prayed and delivered the candles, Jesus gave me a vision. He and I were standing on a mountain looking down at the people below. They were sort of gray, in a gray environment. They were rushing around, busy and worn out looking, and I asked Him if this was

Seattle. It wasn't. "Is it New York?" "Chicago?" "Los Angeles?" He shook His head. Clearly I was on the wrong track. "So, are these people in a big city?" I asked. That's when the scene shifted to a more rural setting, but the environment was still pretty much the same. Same grayish color, same grayish people rushing around, busy, busy, busy. The word "RAT RACE" came to me, and suddenly I understood what I was looking at. There they were, hectic little self-important people, going about their own business faster and faster, and becoming more and more gray. That's when He showed me the little bird like things on the heads and shoulders of each person as they scurried about the streets. The bird things kept pecking at the back of their heads, or tapping on their shoulders as if to push the people still faster. "Hurry, hurry, hurry", their actions seemed to say.

Then suddenly, the coolest thing happened. Each time one of the people would read from the Bible, sing a praise song, help someone out, or offer an encouraging word, even though they remained focused on what they were doing in their world, Jesus showed me what He saw in the spiritual realm. Each time a person had even the smallest thought of God it was a reason to celebrate! A bright golden light would suddenly burst out of them, causing the little bird like creatures to slide down to the person's ankles. Then, though they would still be doing whatever they were doing in the natural realm, in the spiritual realm the people would look up to smile and wave at their Savior! This absolutely delighted Jesus! He laughed so hard He cried, and it was such a JOY to get to witness that with Him! To this day, whenever I start feeling pressured or cranky or some other, all too human, negative mood found in the "rat race," I will stop myself and immediately look up to begin waving and smiling at Jesus. It makes me giggle, especially when I'm driving and I catch somebody in a car alongside mine giving me a funny look. Friends, don't you know He's laughing right along with me? This is my Jesus!

The most important question for you at this point is, Who is Jesus to You?

CHAPTER 4

More Than Enough

Teach those who are rich in this world not to be proud and not to trust in their money, which is so unreliable. Their trust should be in God, who richly gives us all we need for our enjoyment. (1 Tim 6:17 NLT)

Last year I was asked to speak at a large, Girls' Night Out Dinner Event to be held in a church in the Puget Sound Region. *This in of itself was such a lovely God Kiss!* Angie, the ministry team member responsible for selecting the speaker had seen my talk at a small event that February, and now six months later during the planning period, she thought I would be a fun, refreshing choice for the ladies. (Their church's regular goal had been to find clean, humorous presentations for this annual outreach event. However, following a year in which the selected stand-up comic did nothing to point to Jesus, it was agreed that perhaps they needed something that was not only lighthearted, but more heartfelt.) The trouble was, three years had passed since Drawing Water closed its doors, and without a website or active social media presence to view even old videos, the women's ministry team had lots of questions. *Surprisingly to me, it didn't help that we (Drawing Water) had performed at that church for three different Women's Events about a dozen years earlier.* The church had been under different leadership then and the new team were all relatively new to both the church and the community. Abba had a plan though, and when the woman who had seen me speak stuck her neck out in recommending me, the other women on her ministry team decided to trust her enough to agree to the booking.

Angie and I met in August in a coffee shop where she could share with me the specifics planned for the evening. It was to take place two weeks before Thanksgiving, before the usual holiday busyness really took over, and their chosen theme was "Half Full". *Could I ever relate!*

At the time I was literally living somewhere between seasons and halfway between two homes, communities, and family. We had sold our house in June to downsize, but instead of moving to our next forever home, I had organized and moved everything we were keeping to either the little home we bought in Texas, or to the little apartment we were renting locally in the Seattle area. Apartment living was quite an adjustment, and I admit I really struggled with a feeling of restlessness. All of my lists had been checked off; I had completed acting as family moving coordinator and suddenly, I found myself adrift. *Now what, Abba? What should I be doing?* I could still write, or speak, or craft, or… it was really hard for me to focus. Additionally, the mostly young people in our building weren't interested in forging relationships, and traveling back and forth to Texas for short stays hadn't been enough to really build friendships there either. *How could it be possible to have two places to live and yet no real community?* I was spinning.

So, in His goodness, God decided to get my attention. One morning I was heading downstairs in the elevator with our family dog when the elevator gave a sudden lurch and stopped halfway between the third and fourth floors. It was unnerving but not frightening. The lights were on and I could hear the air conditioning running.

There was a call button for help but I decided to try all of the other reasonable options first. No, the elevator wouldn't go up. No, it wouldn't go down. The doors wouldn't open either. It was time to push the alarm. Instantly, there was a recorded message. "You are in Elevator Number 1 located at 184—- (apartment building address)" *Apparently this is important information and presumably it's designed to reassure people who may be panicked while trapped in an elevator. The message repeated 7 or 8 times before a person came on the line.*

The call center attendant asked first about any possible medical emergencies, then about the passengers in the elevator (just my dog and me), and then if I had my phone with me so that he could call back with information later if necessary. *I had no idea my phone would work in the elevator!* Anyway, after our conversation I texted my husband about my predicament and then I decided to sit down for however long the wait might be and scooped up Oreo in my lap. I hope you can already see what I was missing until that point. I had been so focused on doing things on my own I hadn't been truly giving the Lord the time He deserves, and I NEED. Once I started thanking Him for keeping us safe in the elevator, and for the blessing of interim housing, and for having my furry friend with me, and for being able to connect with the "outside world" by cell phone, and so forth and so on, I started laughing... God is SO funny!

After about 40 minutes, I heard a loud clunk above me and a man called down, asking if I was still in the elevator. *(umm... really?)* He told me he would be releasing the doors but that I shouldn't try to open them. Not a problem for me; frankly I wasn't sure I wanted to know if there was something precarious about my situation until help arrived in person. A few more loud noises, one more lurch when he climbed on the roof of the car we were in, and then about 5 minutes later the repairman opened the door. The floor of the elevator car met him about waist high. I handed him Oreo, and then slid on my bottom to the edge of the car, before easing myself down to the actual 3rd floor of the building. Afterwards, the repairman and I took the other elevator down to the lobby where the apartment leasing agent stood waiting. Tim had left him 3 messages and apparently they were both concerned about how I might be coping. There was no need to worry; I'm sure this sounds nutty, but I had my joy back! I had been having a great heart-to-heart with Jesus about what He wanted me to learn and I "got it"—the reminders were loud and clear: 1) No matter how many lists I make, I'm not in control. 2) Abba is ALWAYS with me and for me, and I only need to slow down and reconnect with Him to find my peace. And wouldn't you know, from being stuck halfway between floors I also got a great story for my upcoming talk on **"Half** Full"! Doesn't He just think of EVERYTHING? *Actually, this wasn't the first time the Holy Spirit gave me a funny little personal anecdote to perfectly underscore the theme or focus of my presentation... Note to self: Don't ever agree to give a talk on <u>baring</u> your soul.*

In the week leading up to the Girls' Night Out event that November, the Holy Spirit woke me to reframe, and in some cases, to rewrite my entire talk three times, right up until the morning I was to speak! While I will admit here that as much as I am so thrilled when the Spirit takes over—filling my talks with His thoughts—I do get nervous when all of my careful preparation gets thrown out, and I sometimes find myself initially stumbling over my words. There were over three hundred women gathered at this event, all anticipating a polished performance. The announcer introduced me as "the comedienne," (this is rarely good for those of us who aren't joke-telling, stand-up comics) and I was more than a little surprised to learn the theme title had been changed to "Filling Your Cup." I needn't have worried. **God always equips us completely when He calls us into ministry moments.** My wonderful friend Joeke, acting in a supportive role, had come with me to provide a buffer—allowing me to focus before the talk—and to help distribute contact cards following it. In addition to being one of those people who anticipates needs and knows exactly how to promote and help others, Joeke is one of the wisest and most spiritually discerning people I have ever met. She invited me to her church when she realized our family hadn't yet found a church home in Washington; she invited me to join Bible Study Fellowship when she could see how thirsty I was for a deeper relationship with the Lord, and later she served on Drawing Water's Board of Directors with wisdom and insight. I cannot tell you how much I have appreciated her counsel through the years, and yet that night at the Girls Night Event, most of all I appreciated her for her friendship and selfless love. When I wrapped up the talk and returned to our table, Joeke leaned over to give me a hug of reassurance, and then once the evening was officially dismissed, she visited ladies at other tables to answer questions about future potential bookings, while I greeted several women who wanted to meet me and share part of their story. Once again, some of their favorite highlights were the last-minute revisions the Holy Spirit had me incorporate in the talk that very morning!

I absolutely LOVE living this full out, alive, more than I expect, overflowing, abundant life with Jesus! How about you?

After four years of living in a transitional season which included big moves, job change, and downsizing, I can share with complete authority and confidence that God's best for us is SO MUCH MORE than anything we can dream or imagine. Despite the global hardships of 2020—a year marked by pandemic, economic disaster, civil division and violence in our streets—despite the oppressive blanket of overwhelming fear which has been cast over Believers and Non-Believers alike, let me assure you—if we had all of the stuff in the world that tempts us, it still wouldn't come close to God's true abundant life.

Let me encourage you to expand your perspective as we look at some of the many ways He provides for, and gives favor to us, over and over again, not because we deserve it, but because He is our Faithful Loving Father. Simple examples include having just the right worship song come on the car radio when you need it the most… discovering that you've "accidentally" joined just the right Bible study group that will grow your faith in new ways… meeting a friend at just the right time when they know of an opportunity that would be perfect for you…There are no coincidences, remember?! I know that God introduced me to my faith-filled Sister Friends who encourage me and keep me accountable. And looking back, to the time before I even knew Jesus, He picked out my husband for me. Tim and I were set up on a blind date! Later we discovered that his father and my aunt worked together and were close friends when we were small children. *Today I think Abba set the wheels in motion even back then.*

Over time, one incredible beauty of walking with God appears as we age into new seasons of life. As long as we remain connected to the Vine, He continues to pour fruitfulness into our lives, though the circumstances may look very different than we expect.

Even though God had prepared me, even though my ministry partner Tracie and I were in full agreement, even though our Board of Directors prayerfully came to the same conclusion, I really felt the loss and grieved when it became clear that Drawing Water would be coming to a close. For fourteen years this had been my passion and my life's work. For fourteen years we were so blessed to be able to bless others with this unique calling. Nevertheless, it was obvious that the end was imminent and so I decided to find a part time job to help fill the massive vacancy in my days that would follow once we officially closed the doors of Drawing Water Ministry.

Perhaps you already suspect what happened next? Yes! God went before me and out of the blue, a friend told me about a job opportunity in a local health spa. I applied, was interviewed by phone and in person, and though I had never worked in that industry, I was hired on the spot at the 2nd interview. It was a great fit for me from the start. Hired as a Spa Concierge I would be working part-time in a flexible schedule, in a rotation of three distinct people-oriented positions. At times I would be scheduled as a locker attendant, at other times in reservations, and I would also work at the front desk for guest check in and check out services. I knew it would be the kind of job that would keep me busy at work, but one I could completely put out of my mind when I was off duty. I also knew there would be some fun perks to this position—namely occasional vastly discounted spa services, and a health club membership. What I had no way of knowing is that our Heavenly Father had my ministry heart in mind too!

When 2016 drew to a close, Drawing Water was laid to rest and I was in training for not only the new Spa job, but for an expansion of my purpose as an encourager. My new theme for the next year had been revealed—Partnership with God—and I sensed deep in my spirit that He was telling me, "I'm not finished with you yet." It started happening right away. I knew intuitively that a woman in the locker room needed ice for her knee, and in bringing it, I was able to share my own story and how God had miraculously brought about healing. A mother called me while I was in reservations, needing an immediate haircut for her son from one of our stylists, and digging deeper, I was uniquely able to help her navigate the emotions of watching a child struggle with social issues and bullying. *Later the same day I was asked to trade with one of the concierges on the desk where, meeting this mom in person, I could encourage her further and even give her a recommendation for a good local youth psychologist who had helped my son. God is SO Good!* There was the woman in tears because her son had entered boot camp and wouldn't be home for Christmas… the man who called reservations, desperate to find a way of helping his wife out of her depression… the woman in the locker room who believed that her co-workers only gave her the spa certificate because they felt sorry for her. In almost every shift I worked there would be someone that God would specifically bring to me—whether one of our guests or a fellow employee—proving again and again that ministry success didn't depend on a performance or a large audience. A ministering heart operating with the Spirit's anointing and gifts can share His love anywhere. Also, despite what I previously imagined, people who can afford high end spa treatments have just as many trials and sorrows as the rest of us. Human beings in all ages and stages of life can be wounded, broken, lonely, and troubled. We ALL need God's love.

As often is the case with God's gifts, there would come still another major blessing from following His lead into this part time position in the Spa. Jesus wanted me to not only enrich my purpose, but He wanted me to get to know Giuseppe, *His Healer*. One Friday night when I was working at the desk, I noticed that a cancellation had suddenly occurred opening up a slot in the schedule of one of the most popular, hard-to-get-in-to massage therapists on the staff. The opening caught my attention because I had just had my first conversation with this therapist, Giuseppe, a few days before in an elevator when he told me he had heard I was a Christian and confirmed his own faith. (Believing in Jesus is unusual in this field, especially in the Pacific Northwest where many massage therapists place "healing crystals" under their tables, or follow some sort of eastern spirituality.) I watched and waited to see if the spot would stay open; if a new appointment wasn't booked within 30 minutes before it was to take place, and if it was after my scheduled shift was to end, I could schedule it for myself as a Spa trade. Well, I got the appointment; talk about favor!

When I walked into Giuseppe's massage room my feet were swollen, my shoulders felt heavy, and my right hip throbbed with pain deep within it. From the moment he watched me stand, walk, and then sit on the edge of his table he could see what needed to be done. The massage itself was as skillfully handled as you could imagine in the natural, but in the supernatural, this was a whole different level of physical healing than anything I had ever experienced before. While he worked, Giuseppe prayed out loud over each part of my body the shiatsu massage targeted and I began to feel all kinds of sensations throughout my body. It was almost as if a thick warm oil was flowing through my blood stream and then everything began to vibrate. It literally tickled, and made me laugh, but this wasn't from the massage therapist's external touch; everything was trembling from the inside out—like the molecules which had been all compressed together causing pain, suddenly began dancing into their correct place. *I realize that this sounds unbelievable, but we're talking about God here.* Not only did I walk out of the therapy room that night pain free and more flexible than I had been in years, but the part of my spiritual walk that I had unconsciously put aside for a while woke back up, and I began to see more in the spirit realm again! I'll be sharing more about this in a later chapter, but I wanted to include the basics here because it's important to realize that Jesus desires for us to be completely healed—physically, emotionally, and spiritually too.

Perhaps by now you're thinking that this all sounds good but it seems like I haven't yet addressed the elephant in the room. Namely, you've come to see by example that the "Abundant Life" Jesus brings is about so much more than what's in your bank account, yet the question remains—does God's Abundance include financial resources? The short answer is—YES! God absolutely provides necessities and financial resources to overflowing! My husband and I discovered this fairly early on in our marriage. We started attending a Bible based church and began tithing from the first time we learned that God invites His children to test Him in this way.[xi] It turns out, it's all true—you can't outgive God! I have lots of cool stories—the two new microphones gifted to Drawing Water... the hot tub clearance sale that I "accidentally" found on the sale's final day... An unexpected refund appearing on our credit card statement right when the dentist's bill became due... and so on. When we tithed out of Tim's inheritance from his mother, owners of the out-of-reach, never-in-our-lifetime dream home not only suddenly dropped their asking price by a LOT, but they accepted our offer—this in a Seller's Market. On more than one occasion, God also gave Tim and me the privilege of partnering with Him to bless others. *If you ever feel a nudge to give someone a cash gift, and when you pray about it, the amount to give becomes clear, act on it. I can't express what a blessing it is to know that God has used you to bless someone else with exactly what they need at exactly the right time.* Abba has shown us again and again what a truly extravagant giver He really is!

Just a couple of years ago He shocked us with a financial gift we NEVER saw coming. While we have been blessed through the years, and my husband makes a good living, the Seattle Area is expensive, and I always worked at least part time to help with the extras—things like family vacations, entertaining friends, eating out, and special purchases. When it became clear however that it was necessary for me to leave my job, and that I might not earn much of anything for a while, we expected to once again tighten our belts. Tim and I have been make-do people throughout our marriage. *We were both raised by single moms in working class families (His father passed away when Tim was 10, and my father abandoned our family just after my 14th birthday.)* In every home purchase during our 31 years together, for example, we have prioritized the essentials (replacing the roof), and lived with the previous owners' personal style (from the 1970's avocado tile and wood paneling, to the excessive 1980's wall paper and gold fixtures). The thing was, we also knew we would have some new expenses coming up and soon.

By this point, now several years after my car accident, I experience greater physical challenges than I did when I was younger. As the body ages, it's normal for joints to get stiff and muscles to weaken some, but my earlier injuries have definitely accelerated the process. I had to leave the job as Spa Concierge after just 1 ½ years because I was having great difficulty sitting at a computer for an 8-hour shift in reservations, standing for an 8-hour shift at the front desk, or walking the 7 miles up and down stairs clocked on my fitbit in an 8-hour shift as a locker room attendant. It became so that I literally needed the full day after each of my three weekly work days just for recuperation! A year before contemplating leaving work, these same physical challenges led Tim and me to agree that we would be getting our home ready to sell and move out by the following spring. Our kids were grown; we didn't need so much room, and we had accumulated so much stuff through the years that I actually felt trapped. Between the stairs, and the size, it was too much house for me to maintain well, and we had stopped entertaining. What was once a place of peace had become a burden. The tricky part was that Tim wasn't at retirement age yet. In fact he's still not ready to retire. The idea of selling our big house to move into a smaller, one-level house or condo in the kind of community we wanted to settle in, still in the Seattle area close to Tim's work, made no economic sense—not if we wanted to afford retirement. Added to our financial concerns included my ongoing chiropractic treatments (not covered by our insurance), travel expenses to visit family in the states and our son overseas, and the ongoing support of our younger son who had chosen to go back to school and was living with us.

Trust me when I say, we knew full well how blessed we were already. You don't have to go far in Seattle to see the homeless. What I'm trying to convey here is the frugality in our thinking. Once again we were thinking about what we could do <u>without</u>; instead, Abba wanted us to be free to make decisions not based on the economic bottom line. When the check from the lawyer came, I nearly fell out of my chair. My favorite teacher/dear lifetime friend, Ann had passed away, unexpectedly leaving me an inheritance in her will. I had received the notice months before this, but I didn't really consider what it would mean. At the time I was so saddened to hear of her death, and I was so moved that she would think of leaving me anything, I never questioned what the amount would be. I just assumed coming from a retired teacher it would be a small but lovely gesture from a woman who loved me. As it turned out, when her estate was settled and closed, this unimagined gift was enough to cover moving expenses, some chiropractic visits, a little travel, and even a down payment on our new forever home in TX.

Can you see how the Lord doesn't just throw provision and favor around randomly? He is detailed and specific and ever faithful to the children He loves! He didn't simply bless us with financial resources for our latest move, for example, He picked out our new neighborhood, our church, and even a connection to the community for such a time as this! God knew Covid was coming, and He made sure that I was ready for what could have been an incredibly isolated, frightening time.

We hadn't planned to buy a home in Texas when we came for a visit over Christmas in 2018. We weren't even looking. (Remember, Tim isn't retired and through the course of writing this book, we have lived apart so that he could honor his commitment to remain at his job site in the Seattle Area until the beginning of January 2021.) However, from the first time we visited family there, we loved McKinney; the historic district with its quaint downtown area was exactly the kind of place where we hoped to retire someday. So, one afternoon we decided to drive around a little in the neighborhoods to see what was for sale—just for fun—and to gather information for the future. There was a For Sale sign on a sweet little one story house from the 50's that had recently been renovated, and so we called the realtor for a tour. She heard our story, offered to show us more homes on future visits, and then told us her associate could come over to show us this home. (It had been on the market for a while. There was another interested party, and the price had already been dropped, but the other couple still hadn't made an actual offer.) Anyway, as soon as we entered the home, we knew it would be perfect for us. When, completely out of character, Tim suggested we make an offer, there was an instant affirmation in my spirit. We made the offer and within three weeks, the house was closed and ours! To a person of faith, this is incredibly confirming that we were following God's lead, right? But there's more to the story…

Throughout 2019 I made several visits down to the house in Texas, including a month-long visit in May to receive and move in the furniture we were keeping from our home in Washington. During these visits I began to get to know our immediate neighbors, and one Sunday, I decided to visit a beautiful church nearby that always seemed to be busy with activity. Once again God's orchestration of events just blows me away! It was a very special service that day at First McKinney. Apparently at their last gathering the Pastor had given a very unusual challenge. Each member of the congregation over the age of 5 years that was present in the Worship Center was instructed to <u>take</u> an envelope filled with a $20 bill from the offering plate. Their task would be to pray and see who they could bless in their community. During the week the people wrote in about what they did with the money, and on this particular Sunday, several people were asked to come forward and share their stories. It was Beautiful! All of the stories were touching, but when an 8 or 9 year old boy stood up and told about blessing Miss Heather at the ice cream store *who always remembered his favorite kind and gave him extra sprinkles the year his mama was sick and his grandma watched him after school and took him out for ice cream,* the tears were rolling down my face. The little boy wanted to know if Miss Heather knew about Jesus, and when he gave her the $20. he also invited her over for dinner, just to make sure. THAT is a church I wanted to join. When I helped move our younger son down to the house in December of 2019 I decided to begin attending the First McKinney church services. Tim needed to return to work in Seattle right after Christmas, but we agreed it would be helpful if I remained in Texas for a couple of months to help get our son settled. Anticipating that a real connection with local sisters in Christ would be important for me, I joined a women's small group. Little did we know that soon we would be sheltered in. Zoom calls and prayers with my new small group friends in Heartstrings would become a lifeline. And still there's more!...

On the very day I dropped my husband off at the airport, I wondered what I could do to get to know more of the local community I was suddenly a part of, though I still officially lived in another state. *I'll be talking more about this in a later chapter, but I really sensed that God was telling me it was time to open up one of my "boxes" (important skills or hobbies from my earlier life that I had put away for a time).* I looked online to see if there was a community theatre in the area, and wouldn't you know that God would provide something amazing for me here too? Not only did the local community theatre rehearse and perform less than a mile from my home—an important bonus if my son started working and had the car—but they were having auditions **the next day** for a play in which I was the right age/well-suited for one of the roles! I thought, *Why not throw my hat in the ring? Even if I'm not cast it would be a great opportunity to meet some people locally who enjoy theatre too!* With the audition for the McKinney Repertory Theatre the very next evening, I didn't have time to start second-guessing myself; I just cobbled together a basic resume, found an old photo (It has been YEARS since I needed a head shot) and showed up at the open call. To be sure, I was rusty and it was not one of my best auditions. In fact, when the director phoned me a few days later, I asked her if she'd like to meet socially sometime for dinner before one of her rehearsals—figuring this was just a courtesy call and I hadn't been cast. I was genuinely surprised that she was calling to offer me a role, and thus began my first theatrical experience in Texas. Over the course of rehearsals and the run of the show I came to know this new community and its marvelous cast and crew. Additionally, friends I had recently met from church and from my neighborhood graciously came to one of my performances. Truly, our new house in Texas was HOME, and that was very comforting when in the very week after our final performance of the play—a farce which included spit takes and where, after the curtain call each night we would all shake hands with audience members—Texas began sheltering in.

One final thought about God's amazing provision and favor: Be careful that you don't let the regular stuff of your daily life get in the way of your experiencing the supernatural, more than can be imagined LIFE Jesus came to give you! In prior years with our fast paced, busy lives, it became easier and easier to focus on the minutia and miss God's blessings. This year, even though many things may have screeched to a halt and people have found all kinds of "down time to fill", fear and frustration have taken up residence where hope, peace, and joy should be. **Choose instead to look for God's bigger, richer, fullness of life!**

CHAPTER 5

He Makes Things New

I will repay you for the years the locusts have eaten.
(Joel 2:25 NIV)

How are you with waiting? If we're honest, most of us aren't comfortable with it. We like to be busy. We like to be in control. I've had a lengthy transitional, in-between season that has cured me of the naive belief that I am in control of anything! Over the last 4 years, I've had a lot of time to lean in to Jesus, and I've learned a lot. Admittedly at times I probably reminded our Heavenly Father of a stubborn 3-yr-old seated in a grocery cart who reaches for the jelly jar on the store shelf yelling, "Me do it!" *Smash!* Accidentally dropping the jar, the jelly splashes everywhere, and sheepishly I realize I've made a mess of things again. Most of the time, thankfully, I've put aside my agenda and determined instead to listen and reflect, to wait patiently, learning and growing during this period while the seeds of future things lay hidden under the soil. God has blessed me over and over again in His perfect timing. Remember, bread doesn't rise without the time to proof (I'm a big fan of the "Great British Baking Show".) Likewise, this abundant life promised us can't be rushed. *I know it sounds hard. You might even be tempted to think of God as unfeeling or uncaring when you're suffering in the present, but that couldn't be further from the truth.* God's timing isn't ours, but it IS just the right time. You can count on it! The Lord's perfect timing not only applies to provision as I shared in the last chapter, but also to redemption, and to restoration of things lost, or seemingly irreparably damaged.

I know I've already mentioned a little bit about my difficult childhood and the emotional healing that took place after I had begun to follow Jesus wholeheartedly. *Looking back, I can only imagine how hard it would have been, if not impossible, to try to come to terms with that kind of pain without a belief in a loving God.* I remember the time my counselor asked me what I did for fun and I couldn't think of an answer. I had to grow up fast after my dad left us, and my childhood was lost in the wake. For me, everything was about work, responsibility, care-giving, and pressure. While I am the kind of person who gets great satisfaction from producing things, there was ALWAYS an underlying objective to be met or someone to please. I still felt unworthy, remember, and I thought it was too selfish of me to think of *playing* when others were counting on me. Thankfully, after that first big breakthrough when I discovered Jesus' genuine, bottomless love for me, other lessons and God's truth came quickly. I think it was only two counseling sessions later when I reported the revelation I was given during a Drawing Water performance presented that week: God had redeemed my childhood for me! My FUN was on stage! All of the preparations— script writing, rehearsals, costuming, contracts—all of these things were satisfying, but still a task to be done. But on stage, during live performance where anything can happen, I was free to PLAY with childlike abandon. Soon afterwards, my counselor and I agreed that I had crossed over from depression to joy, and our time together came to an end. And wouldn't you know, with a new richness of understanding and having experienced recovery from old baggage, I also began to bring new material, new life to Drawing Water, and our ministry changed for the better. My partner Tracie had also been on a healing journey of her own—*Do you see God's perfect timing here?* So we naturally started sharing about healing and restoration and "God Kisses" when we took time near the end of our programs to speak from our hearts. Still, I never anticipated how one day, Abba would use one of these kisses to affirm and confirm this significant discovery.

We were on a family vacation in Hawaii when I "happened" upon a young girl and her mother selling homemade jewelry. I was instantly drawn to these fun, beaded bracelets strung with elastic. Other tourists must have liked them too   she only had three left. Their primary color was the blue we used in our Drawing Water promotional materials, and I thought they would be a colorful, durable matching wardrobe piece to add to our basic black costumes and an appropriate present for my two friends in the trenches with me during that ministry season. Each of the three bracelets were similar with several common beads and in design and style, but each had a few unique elements as well. The one I selected for my partner, Tracie, had a bead with a jeweled heart. One of those beautiful, rare people who can be both outrageously outgoing, and also so vulnerable as to wear her heart on her sleeve, Tracie still finds "love letters" from God in the heart-shaped rocks she finds on nearly every beach walk to this day. For Jan, performing in an associate role for the season, I chose the bracelet which had a unique star shaped bead. She was so willing to go the extra mile, to do anything we asked of her, and in this little ministry on a shoestring budget, we asked a lot of each of us—with very little tangible reward.

Now the third bracelet, the one left for me didn't have anything particularly special about it at all. I wanted my friends to have the special ones—to have bracelets that would mean something to them beyond just being a costume piece. Like the others, mine was colorful and fun (and not too expensive for me to afford three of them). However, it had this one bead that was kind of a weird, unattractive, lumpy sort of thing. In fact, for the first two months I wore it, I kept trying to maneuver the bracelet on my wrist so that I wouldn't have to see it. Silly me; nothing is ever an "accident" with God. One day I put the bracelet on before a performance and discovered the most remarkable thing; apparently I had been wearing it upside down. That lumpy weird bead was actually Mr. Potato Head! I laughed and rejoiced at the wonder of it. Not only had God preserved my childhood for me on the stage, but here, in this little bracelet, He gave me a token reminding me of the playground He picked out just for me!

The longer I've walked with Jesus, the more I can see how He walked with me before I knew Him. *Is there anything more life-affirming than to know in the very center of your being the extraordinary ways He has Loved and cared for you from the beginning?* In this next story I share a dream in which He both prepared me for a coming loss, AND promised ultimate restoration.

In the dream, I was in the living room of my house (and no it didn't look like my actual home, but that's not the point.) The hardwood floors were gleaming, the windows were spotless and even the walls seemed to have a beautiful golden lustre to them. Unlike other "house" dreams I've had however, this living room was empty. There were no furnishings, no wall decorations, nothing to get in the way of what I saw out the window. In the driveway parked next to the living room rested a small, sporty, silver-colored car that had obviously seen better days. A little two-seater that had clearly once been a little showy and a fun ride, now looked tired and forlorn. The leather on the seats was cracking, the dashboard had faded in the sun, and the tires looked as though they were balding. The once shiny finish had dulled and I remember wondering if it could still go the distance required of it.

Just then, the emergency brake gave way and the car began to roll forward towards the end of the driveway. I watched it, not fully believing what I was seeing, but I didn't do anything to stop it. Instead, I just stood there at the window, watching the well-worn sports car pick up speed. It was incomprehensible. Why was the car rolling away? Suddenly I noticed the driveway was sloped down towards the edge of a cliff! Even more unsettling, as the car rolled past the house, the house too began sliding forward down the slope, as though tethered to the little car. I became alarmed as I realized, I didn't have anything, any way to stop the escaping car. As I watched with shock, the sporty car became suspended as its front wheels hung off the cliff and it began a slow slide on its belly towards ultimately falling off the edge. The house too, now precariously balanced on the side of the cliff, so I madly raced for the opposite side of the house, hoping to somehow counter-balance the pull of the car.

The car finally fell off the cliff, and for a quick, sickening moment, the house seemed to follow suit. But then in a matter of seconds the house landed, still right side up, just about eight feet lower than it had been before. The living room was now underground, like a basement, only it was no longer empty. Now there were boxes, lots and lots of neatly stacked cardboard moving boxes. I had the sense that these were things that were kept for me from my past, important lessons, gifts and treasures that I could put to use again. All I had to do was to figure out how to get these boxes back up above ground… That's when I woke up.

From the time I had the dream in the summer of 2013 I knew that God was showing me an ending of Drawing Water as it had been rolling along. The "sporty little two-seater" was indeed fading as personal problems required Tracie to step back some, and hoping to keep our ministry upright, I took on the full weight of what was always intended to be an equal partnership. In the beginning however, there wasn't absolute clarity on the content of the boxes from the dream, and I didn't realize Abba was actually preparing me for the end of Drawing Water. For the next 2½ years, Tracie and I and our Board of Directors prayed and came to believe that a new focus would revive our operations. Understand, none of us had been released yet from this unique calling. In 2014 divine inspiration fell afresh on our whole group—to create a program that would minister to women in the military and the wives of military personnel—and a new ministry branch, Courageous One was born. Within 2 weeks, just as had occurred in the time leading up to Drawing Water, Abba again gave me a massive download, not just for one program but for 4 consecutive programs. Excitedly we moved forward, imagining new life for our ministry for years to come. Although clearly, that wasn't His plan, the Lord did bless us mightily as we obeyed what we believed was the new calling, and a few hundred women who participated in the birthing process were deeply touched.

In the final performance of Courageous One, for the women at a joint base in Western Washington, we had a number of obstacles to overcome to even present our program. While I'll be discussing spiritual opposition in more detail in another chapter, I can honestly say that never have I seen anything like the efforts of the enemy to keep THIS particular event from happening. Not only were there unexpected personality issues unbecoming of military personnel (lies, slander, fear, indecisive waffling, threats to junior leaders), constant changes to schedule, staffing, venue and level of support, demands for multiple in-person meetings leading up to the event, (unheard of for our ministry or any ministry offering FREE services), but then a fierce winter storm suddenly appeared in the forecast forcing the early closure of the base, nearly cancelling the program. Now I don't know what more would have occurred that night, had our attendance been what was originally planned. However, I do know the Lord had a very special blessing of reconciliation for the 70 +women who did participate that evening.

Our program theme was "You Are Not Alone", and the event was designed to help the women see God in their lives and to connect with their own community. *In a nutshell: by and large on military bases women who serve and wives of servicemen do not associate with one another. The military life is stressful and quite hard on marriages. The women are often lonely and troubled, but afraid to take advantage of community services that might put them in a poor light, or keep their serviceman from promotion.* However, through years of recovery work and by sharing what we were learning with our Drawing Water audiences, Tracie and I had discovered that one thing that can really help people with hidden shame and emotional healing is to know that others have also experienced the same thing. It validates their pain and gives hope for true healing. So, this first Courageous One program was designed to build to a climax we called the scarf wall. Essentially, after trust with us had been established, the women were invited to take a scarf or scarves that represented different common roots of pain that had occurred in their lives—without having to get personal or share their story with anyone—and to just place it on the scarf wall. One color represented sexual assault, another abandonment, another physical abuse or threat, another betrayal by a woman, and one an "unnamed" pain—whether they had fully identified it or not. *(Towards the end of the program this visual became a teaching tool as we talked about healing and how God makes beauty from ashes.)*

During each of the Courageous One performances, the scarf wall moment was profoundly moving. In every audience, women would make their way forward, often putting multiple scarves on the prepared surface. Some would tear up, some would physically stand in support of their friends or relatives… It was always sacred. It was always impactful to not only the women participating, but to our technical crew of local volunteers – usually males – astonished by the numbers of scarves posted in every color, having had *no idea* that so many women—women they knew—ever carried this pain. During this final performance of Courageous One, in the show that nearly didn't happen, the scarf wall undid us all. The women in the audience literally ran down the aisles to participate. We watched women who preferred to isolate from one another at the beginning of the program, now gather together as they held the same color scarves. We saw the former strangers make their way across the auditorium to embrace crying women and gently help them mount their scarf. We saw emotional walls and barriers between the women crumble, as the scarf wall filled in fully. As only God can do, we saw the foundations of reconciliation as this precious community began to come together for perhaps the first time. *Nothing we ever do for God is wasted.*

I've already touched on the grieving process that I went through when Drawing Water Ministry closed its doors at the end of 2016. Interestingly, in the same way as some are prone to discover when a loved one dies, there were things to sort through immediately, and other things to leave boxed up for a later time. This happens both in the physical and in the spiritual realm. Once in a while I wondered about those stacked boxes from what I began to call my Drawing Water farewell dream, but every time I tried to examine them more closely, I had the sense that God wanted me to wait to open them in His perfect timing. Just after I moved my son to Texas, I heard two things at the very beginning of this year (2020): The first was from Proverbs—She is clothed with strength and dignity. She laughs with no fear of the future.[xii] *Wow! Talk about a timely message for 2020! I can't tell you how much this Word has buoyed me in this season when fear seems to be winning on all sides.* The second thing I heard in my spirit was that it was time to begin opening the boxes from that old dream. I've already mentioned my first box—getting involved in theatre in my new community in Texas. (Can you guess what was in the next one?)

Still, the most remarkable story in my life illustrating God's ongoing desire to restore His children answers a question you might be wondering by now—If my husband and I both grew up in California and then later moved to the Seattle area, what prompted the move from the West Coast to Texas? The short answer is, we moved to be closer to my Pop. *Are your sneakers laced up? This story is going to blow your socks off!*

To backtrack a little for context:

In the fall of 2015 I thought it would be fun to take the Ancestry DNA test "just to see what happens." *I had been adopted as an infant and though there was a brief story given by my birth mother about my origins, this all took place back in a time of sealed records and a strict code of privacy for all involved parties.* Anyway, when the kit came, I had no reservations about spitting into the test tube to send off my sample.

I already knew that by human standards, I had been an accident. Whatever ethnic groups or family clans… whatever bad choices my blood ancestors had made… none of this had any bearing on who I am as a person. I wasn't an accident to my Heavenly Father and in this experience too, I knew He'd be with me. Nearly a decade and a half since I lost my mom to Alzheimer's, and a few months after I lost my dad (who hadn't been present in my life for years), it seemed like a good time to explore the concept of biological family in a new way. Besides, ancestry research was really taking off, thanks to the amazing breakthrough discoveries that were happening with DNA.

When the results came back it was really fun! There were percentages of ethnic mixes, and maps and stories of the migration of people groups and where they first settled in the "new world." Suddenly I had HUNDREDS of distant cousins, some with very large, fully fleshed- out family trees. If one of these was listed as a 2nd or 3rd cousin, I figured I could be pretty certain that 1 of their 8 great grandparents was also one of my direct ancestors. I also have to admit that I enjoyed a sense of place and belonging to the human family in a way I hadn't experienced before. *I will be the first to tell you I have struggled with abandonment issues in my past until I received full healing in this area; maybe most adopted children have a taste of this to some degree.* Still, this developing sense of place, of belonging was new and noticeable.

Initially, I sent a few messages to relatives listed with "extremely high" probability of being 1st or 2nd cousins. Perhaps one of them had heard a rumor of Grandma or Auntie giving a baby up for adoption? Eventually however, I realized that without a family surname, I wasn't going to get any further in my search. Unless a sibling just happened to join Ancestry and spit in a test tube, I had come to the end of the road of what I could accomplish, and I stopped checking in to the site. Yet, to actually go in and remove my membership hovered under my radar. I'd see the $20 billed each month for access to their records, and think, "I really should find out how to take care of that," but then I never seemed to get around to it. *Another happy "coincidence"? I think not. Our God is in the miracle business!*

So, one Sunday in late February of 2018 when I knew I would soon be leaving my job at the Spa and the money I was making for little "extras" would come to an end, the $20 charge from Ancestry on my credit card statement jumped out as an obvious budget item to eliminate.

I opened my profile on the Ancestry website and went straight to the DNA tab. I figured, I should at least gather what information I still could before cancelling my membership. I clicked on DNA matches to get a last glimpse of the legions of cousins that continued to populate my profile, when something new caught my eye at the very top of the page. Listed was a "Parent/Child Relationship" marked with "extremely high" likelihood of being an "immediate family member." It was the sentence below this that blew me away: Elliott Davis is your father.

WHAT??!! I remember staring, just staring at this piece of news trying to wrap my mind around it. There was always a possibility that a close relative would one day show up, but a father??? What kind of surprise would this be for him? *I kept thinking about those old black and white T.V. shows where the father to be is pacing in a hospital waiting room and someone hands him a cigar and says, "Congratulations! You have a baby girl (or a baby boy)!" Now here comes Ancestry saying in effect, "Congratulations, Mr. Davis! You have a middle-aged woman!"*

I knew I needed to contact him—this stranger who might be able to fill in so many unknown gaps in my story. But what do you say? And, if I had been the unplanned result of an extra marital affair, would my messaging this person blow up his life? Furthermore, was I prepared to deal with whatever new extended family drama might come my way from this contact? I finally went with a very simple, but straightforward message on the Ancestry site that I hoped would be received well. Either way, there was nothing more to do but wait. *Tim and I were cautiously excited—this is once in a lifetime kind of news—suddenly there were SO many questions... So many possibilities... Of course at the time, we had NO IDEA what impact this all would have on our lives.*

Time just seemed to fly by on that Monday morning at work. As the opening Hostess in the Spa, I began my shift at 6 am and was responsible for among other things, setting up the two women's lounge snack & water stations, making coffee, and ensuring we were well-supplied with folded clean robes and towels from the laundry. The day moved fast, and true to form, I had already hit 10,000 steps by the time most people were just getting started in their day. But unlike any previous Monday, I had two thoughts running through my mind that totally energized me throughout my entire shift—the first was that I wouldn't be doing this physically fatiguing job much longer; the second was that I might hear from my newly found father soon! I think I literally grinned from ear to ear all day, and I KNOW I was telling everyone about this amazing news. I told a few of our regular guests... I told the front desk crew and the Spa providers I came in contact with during my duties for the day... I told the café baristas and a couple of the health club greeters when I went to retrieve drink orders. It was funny—everyone wanted to know more about my story. We had all seen those T.V. shows where long lost relatives reunite; even my co-workers who weren't particularly close with me, genuinely hoped for a happy ending! *A beautiful example of life the way God designed it—Even in the middle of a broken world, we all recognize in the depths of our souls that we were created for love and connection and belonging.*

As excited as everyone was, I still tried to keep my emotions in check. With even the best case scenario, there might be a long waiting period before I even heard from this new relative. (Remember, all messages had to go through the Ancestry site—what if he didn't check his messages very often?) There would also be the possibility of complete rejection. *How would I feel if I never received an answer, or if one came back denying the possibility that I could be his daughter?* As I completed my work and drove home, I focused on trying not to get too carried away. Though this newly identified stranger and I were related, it didn't mean we would ever have an actual relationship. Besides, I knew that Abba is my Father. He loves me and He is always faithful! Perhaps it was all the excitement of the day, or simply the addition of the emotional component to my usually physically exhausting job, but I hit the pillow early and slept soundly all night. *I slept, when in another part of the country somebody else was suddenly wide awake!! But that's his story to tell.*

When Tim rose at o'dark early for work the next morning, I could see that there was a message waiting for me on my phone. It occurred to me that MAYBE, it was something from my new father, but I decided to wait until I was really awake (and it was <u>really</u> morning) before checking it. Again, I didn't want to wake myself up at 3:30 in the morning to be disappointed. So around 7 am on that Tuesday morning, I listened to the message, and I heard his voice for the very first time. WOW. This was it. *Now what????* I listened to the message a few more times, and then went to the Ancestry site to discover, sure enough, there was a sweet reply to my message there too! It was time for me to make the next move. (gulp) I fixed my morning coffee, prayed, took a deep breath, and called him back.

How do you tell the story of your entire life in a phone call? As my Pop and I found out, you can't. Not in 2 calls, or 10, or with a host of emails, or by friending each other on Facebook to share photos. What you CAN do, however, is to discover an amazing, undeniable connection. You CAN move forward with understanding and love. Together, and with a mutual love for Jesus that recognizes His restoration power, you CAN create a whole new shared life.

Pop and his wife—the beautiful woman we affectionately call our Bonus Mom, Betty—live in McKinney, TX. It was on our first visit there over Father's Day Weekend, that Tim and I realized that this Texas town had everything we had been looking for in our future retirement.

Still, the story wouldn't be complete without filling you in on some of the miraculous discoveries we have made along the way. One of the first, and to me, the most revealing of God's intentional designs for each one of us has to do with the uncanny similarities between my biological father and my adopted father. Both men were raised in Virginia in fairly dysfunctional families. Both left home at an early age to join the Navy during wartime. *My dad served in Korea and Pop served in Vietnam.* Both met women who would play a significant role in my life at USO dances. Dad met my adopted mom in San Francisco in the 50's, and Pop met my biological mother in San Diego in the 60's. Both men also experienced problems associated with the after-effects of war, and both blew up their respective families, leaving gaping wounds behind. However, where my adopted dad never received Christ, never got healing, and remained abusive until the end, Pop did find Jesus and recovery—healing physical, emotional, and spiritual trauma. Although Pop and I weren't a part of each other's actual baggage, I can't tell you how freeing it was for both of us when he looked me in the eyes to say how sorry he was for his mistakes as a father, and I looked him in the eyes with complete forgiveness as his child. Abba turned our holes into wholeness, and restored what FATHER really means. Today, I call him Pop, he calls me his Number 1 daughter, and a beautiful relationship also exists between him and Tim, and between this new Grandpa and each of our sons.

Our story also illustrates the amazing ways God will go above and beyond to answer prayer. Unbeknownst to me, my dear friend Kelly began earnestly and regularly praying for me to find genuine family connection from the time I submitted my DNA for testing. Kelly and I had been besties for years, having met as soccer moms in Seattle, and continuing our relationship via weekly Facetime coffee calls and annual girls' weekend trips since she moved to northern Texas 10 years ago. Though Kelly and I are true sisters in Christ who lift each other up continuously with God stories and mutual accountability, never in our wildest dreams did the two of us think we'd end up living near one another again! *Of all places to find someone she had been praying for me to find—God is SO Good!*

Next, in one of those marvelous non-coincidental, God Kisses, there's the timing of the Ancestry announcement itself. As I mentioned before, had I cancelled my membership earlier, I might not have ever seen this newly identified relationship. I wouldn't have gone on the site to look for it. Likewise, Pop nearly missed my message to him. The night he read it he himself was going on Ancestry to cancel his membership! (He had entered his DNA out of curiosity about an ethnic question; it never occurred to him that there might be a new relative from out of the blue.)

Today, we are all so grateful for the way God used this tool to bring us together! Years after Tim and I both lost our parents and our kids lost their grandparents, we have the amazing opportunity to restore the years the locusts have eaten out of our family life. Now living in our sweet home in McKinney, just 3 miles from Pop and Betty, I have the privilege of joining my father for coffee/breakfast every Tuesday, Tim and Pop enjoy guy things/common interests every chance they can get, and we have family dinner and game nights every weekend.

Finally, we all have a GREAT story to tell about our Great Big God and the Great Big Life He has for us, everywhere we go. With the connection to Ancestry.com and all of the shows on television these days about finding your roots or finding long lost loves, this is a really easy story to share with everyone—insurance agents, tax preparers, sales clerks, postal carriers, strangers on airplanes, you name it! Once again, the best stories aren't really about us at all; maybe they're not even for us, but for the others whom we can bless.

Friends, (and if you've followed along with me this far through these stories, you certainly are friends!) if I can encourage you with one very special reminder, let it be this:

For everything in this past year that has been stolen from you, for everything the enemy meant to use for your harm—for the dreams crushed, the relationships torn apart, the lives lost, and the divisions that continue to threaten the fabric of civilization itself— our Almighty God is in control! In His perfect timing and with His amazing goodness and mercy, He WILL restore and redeem what has been taken. Fear Not!

*Everything I've taught you is so that the peace which is in me will be in you and will give you great confidence as you rest in me. For in this unbelieving world you will experience trouble and sorrows, **but you must be courageous, for I have conquered the world!*** (John 16:33 TPT)

CHAPTER 6

Doing Life With Jesus

I pray that the Father of glory, the God of our Lord
Jesus Christ, would impart to you the riches of the
Spirit of wisdom and the Spirit of revelation to know
Him through your deepening intimacy with Him.
(Eph 1:17 TPT)

The other night I woke up with spinning thoughts. It's been
a challenging season on so many levels, but I knew what to
do to get back to sleep. I have made it a habit to follow the advice
from the scripture I painted around the ceiling of our home office
space. I work to fix my thoughts on good things, things that deserve
praise. *Is whatever stray thought that is keeping me awake even true,
or right, or worthy of my time and attention?* Or, say I'm stewing
about a disagreement with someone; can I focus on the best or the
beautiful about them, instead of the irritating or ugly parts? God
brings peace to us when we intentionally redirect our thoughts in
this way![xiii] Moreover, I have found that as soon as I start reciting
these verses during the night hours, Abba in His Goodness never
lets me down. On this particular night, I started reciting scripture

that I have internalized over the years, and I was so comforted to know there was a lot of it! *I can't say that I've ever been particularly good about sitting down to memorize Bible verses or knowing their exact location. However, through worship song lyrics, and years of Bible study, through emotional recovery work, journaling regularly, and even writing and performing Drawing Water sketches that relied heavily on the use of scripture, I am so grateful to be able to stand on God's Word when I'm distressed or exhausted.* Anyway, after reciting some of my favorite verses out loud, and then still more in my head, I don't know if I was starting to fall asleep and dream at this point, but my middle of the night processing wasn't complete quite yet. There was a shift and it was almost as if I was a contestant on a game show where I both asked and answered several Bible knowledge-based questions. "Where would you find the Hall of Faith?" (Hebrews) "Where would you find a reference to God's divine plans and the first time the phrase, *'For such a time as this'* was used?" (the Book of Esther) "Where can you learn about the pieces of God's armor given to Believers?" (Ephesians) I realize that this may sound silly, but each time I correctly answered my own questions, bells and lights would go off and there would be cheering. I don't really know how long this entire mental exercise took—fixing my thoughts, etc.—but I can tell you I fell asleep soundly with such peace and total assurance of my identity as His beloved daughter.

In many ways, together, you and I have now reached the heart or climax of this book of stories. If you're to make the leap and receive for yourself this Abundant Life that Jesus came to give you, this life that is full, exciting, and joyful—no matter what earthly circumstances you find yourself in—You're going to have to do your part. Do you WANT a personal, vibrant relationship with Jesus of your very own? This is about so much more than merely asking Him to be your Savior and going to church on Sundays! While it's true that the Lord rescues and heals, provides, protects, and restores as I've shared in previous chapters, and while you may certainly experience the miraculous (I pray that you do!), I think most of our walk when we're fully alive with Jesus comes from learning to recognize His daily presence. He is in the little things too—the whispers of encouragement, the divine God kisses that should never be chalked up to simply "coincidence," the aha's of confirmation when something you hear on the radio connects with a Sermon message, which relates to a dream you had, which correlates to a truth unwittingly shared by your neighborhood mail carrier. God is WITH you and FOR you. In your heart of hearts, do you know this to be true?

What follows is a collection of short stories of ways that I've seen my faith grow over the years through the more usual kinds of God encounters and interactions that occur in daily life, and the evidence I hold dear about my own close connection with the Lord.

From the very beginning of when I turned my life over to Jesus, I knew that a genuine, life-changing faith would require my total commitment. However, it was also true that like many of you reading this, at the time my life was stretched beyond busy. I was a young mother with a pre-schooler and an infant when my own mother—diagnosed with Alzheimer's—moved in with us. Then, in part because my husband's salary couldn't adequately support the five of us in Southern California where we lived, I went to work full time as a 6th grade teacher. I had a LOT on my plate. Now, awakened with the Spirit, I looked forward to one day participating more in church activities, to serving regularly and to learning more about my Savior, but for the time being, I wasn't sure how I could fit in one more thing. *Silly me.* **God knows our hearts, and He will always make a way for His children to get to know Him better!** An opportunity came up at Christmas time to serve in a remarkable ministry event at my church, which in effect created an interactive, outdoor "Bethlehem" for the public. I've never seen an outreach event quite like it before or since, but this was the perfect way for me—with my drama background, and with no time for rehearsal—to participate fully alongside a well-organized, fun-loving and faithful team. I was cast as one of the food vendors "selling" figs and dates for the "shekels" (metal washers) the tourists were given to spend. I loved every minute of it—from the first meet and greet where we were assigned costumes and learned how the village worked, to setting up the marketplace each night with awnings, props, and the like, to the group prayer before each presentation, to interacting with the thousands of people who came to "Bethlehem" during our five-night run. While I realize the Bethlehem Ministry event was for everyone who came and participated, God was SO good to me, new Believer that I was!

It was there I first learned of the power of praying out loud with others, and where I first heard examples of others' prayers. *They didn't have to be formal as I thought; these were just expectant conversations with our loving Father.* **It was also where I saw firsthand prayers answered miraculously!** The Bethlehem Village was set up on the little hillside and in the field just below the church. The church itself was in the Santa Susana mountains, just off the 118 Freeway. The event planners could count on reasonable temperatures for an outdoor activity in December, but the wind through the mountain passes was highly unpredictable. On the last two presentation evenings, strong wind gusts started whipping up the canvas tent awnings, threatening our cancellation just before "Bethlehem" was to open to the public. Our team held hands and prayed that the Lord would hold the wind back. Both nights, the winds calmed down as quickly as they started. We opened the village and celebrated with the evening's visitors. Then, both nights, as the last guests passed by the Wisemen's camp exiting "Bethlehem," the winds picked back up in full force! *We know the One who can calm the storms!*

A few years later when we moved to the Seattle area, my children were both in school, my mother had moved into an assisted living facility with an Alzheimer's unit, and I was invited to join a group of women neighbors in my first ever Bible study. The five of us met in a woman's home and each week we'd share things we had noticed from our daily readings from the study Bible we were using, the <u>Change</u>

Your Life Daily Bible.[xiv] The woman facilitating our discussions had heard of this special edition—a New Living Translation comprised of Old Testament, New Testament, Psalms, and Proverbs organized into 365 daily readings—and thought it would be an excellent tool for both the inexperienced and more mature Believers within our group. It was astonishing! **Even though I was a newbie and probably didn't "get" half of what I was reading, because of this intentional pairing of scripture I could see the connections between the Old and New Testaments; I could grasp how together, God's story unfolds from first to last, unchanging.** For example, on the same day I read about the laws in Leviticus of a woman being "unclean" after giving birth or while on her menstrual period—and the purification, or atonement that must occur before she could join community life in the synagogue again—there was the story in Mark about Jesus healing the woman with the bleeding issue when she reached out and touched the hem of His robe. *Jesus answered the Law's requirements down to the smallest detail.* Then as if to highlight the connections I was making, the cries of Psalm 38—part of the same day's reading assignment—practically jumped off the page! Vs 8—"I am exhausted and completely crushed. My groans come from an anguished heart." Vs 11—"My loved ones and friends stay away, fearing my disease. Even my own family stands at a distance." Vs 21—"Do not abandon me, Lord. Do not stand at a distance, my God."(NLT)

This first Bible study experience was also significant in that it showed me how different translations could completely change and deepen my understanding. I'll never forget the first time I read the 23rd Psalm in the New Living Translation. Verse 6 says, "Surely your goodness and unfailing love will pursue me all the days of my life." Pursue? That one little word, the one I had always seen as "follow me," forever changed my thoughts about God's enormous longing for relationship with mankind! *Some translations are better for a word by word study, others attempt to achieve the same emotional engagement as was found in the original texts. Taken together* *they give us a more complete picture of God's meaning and purpose. I'm old school and prefer having actual written pages to turn, writing notes in the margins and looking at them side by side. But there are wonderful online versions of the Bible where you can get multiple translations of a verse or chapter with a click of a button. Go ahead and explore. You might be really surprised by something you've never seen before!*

Each week as the women in our group all shared different things based on their season of life or prior experience with the Word, I realized why group study can be so valuable. Not only did they have scripture insights that I never would have noticed, but these women gave beautiful examples of different ways to pray, and wonderful Christian parenting advice. **As God's people, we are meant to do life together.** I was also thrilled to discover that every person, from the newest to the most experienced, can make valuable contributions to the whole group! I'll never forget when the more spiritually mature Believers in my first Bible study small group shared that my practice of reading Bible passages aloud—using my familiar theatrical training to put myself in the role of the various characters—often revealed a truth or a lesson in scripture that they had never seen. With different backgrounds, personalities, spiritual gifts and talents, every person fulfilling his or her purpose is essential for the health of the whole body. Paul talks about Jesus' followers in the Church as parts of an actual physical body—a hand, an eye, and even hidden parts that are usually covered.[xv] Over the years I've seen where frequently in Christian circles, people will joke about being the spleen or the little toe, but the reality is, God designed his master creation perfectly. Somewhere along the way in my studies, the Holy Spirit gave me a little mini-vision of Believers being like the shards of a mirror. Only by putting all the shards together can we see the true and total reflection of who Jesus is.

Intentionally gathering in a small group or fellowship to talk about the things of God is by far one of the greatest gifts you can give yourself. From this very first circle of neighborhood ladies to the small groups assigned through my years in BSF (Bible

Study Fellowship), to the years of church home fellowships and the wonderfully engaging discussions even welcomed through a variety of formal Bible study classes, to friends and peers working alongside in service opportunities or in recovery groups, I have learned that there is nothing like growing and gleaning Christian lifestyle principles from other Believers, sharpening one another with the Word to build and fortify your faith. Today, one of my heart prayers is that in the same way, I will mentor others with the same kind of wisdom and humor that was so graciously given to me. That by sharing my struggles and successes I too can offer helpful suggestions about this most important Spiritual journey—perhaps with ideas to establish a consistent Quiet Time with God, or by offering life experiential insights on maintaining healthy boundaries with others.

I realize that you and I may have very different lives, so please understand that I'm not trying to be prescriptive here about your faith. There is not a one-size fits all approach to achieving intimacy with Jesus and experiencing His abundance. However, I can't write a chapter like this without expressing a serious caution: Because scripture teaches who God is and who we are to Him, naturally the enemy will try everything he can to distract us or dissuade us from knowing God's Word. If you genuinely can't fit a group or class into your schedule, (*no judgment- I've been there!*) you can still ask the Spirit for help to carve out a few minutes each day for your growing relationship. There are many wonderful resources that teach God's Truth in manageable daily doses. *When I was first introduced to self-study through devotionals, Sarah Young's* <u>Jesus Calling</u>[xvi] *was so popular it could be found on Costco pallets. I have since re-read this book and given it as a gift many times through the years. My new favorite resource for daily reading is Jonathan Cahn's* <u>The Book of Mysteries</u>.[xvii] *While I am very familiar with God's Word at this point in my journey, I have been learning SO Much from the deeper understanding that comes from the original Hebrew and Jewish traditions only a Messianic Rabbi could share.*

Sometimes growth is such a slow process we don't see it while it's happening. Then one day, as we look back we can see how "suddenly" we are well on our way to becoming the person God created us to be!xviiiFor me, to be able to fully claim my identity as a child of God without even the smallest shred of doubt has brought such JOY and PEACE. But there is a cost: it can also be a surprise when you realize **you may have to actively remove things from your life that no longer align with the new person you are becoming in Christ.** Just about the time I could recognize actual growth in my faith—talking with Jesus and hearing from Him in my Spirit was becoming more and more natural and consistent—I began to see that things like the movies and T.V. programs I used to enjoy began to upset me and disturb my sleep at night. By this point, Abba was teaching me about discerning real evil in the world, and so these fictional stories were no longer entertaining to me, but tragic and horrifying. It was a difficult adjustment for my husband and our sons too—Suddenly Mom couldn't go to many movies with the family or watch family favorites on television. *Again, I'm not saying this kind of entertainment is bad, it was just clearly bad for ME.* Perhaps one day, dark visual stimulus and the excessive use of foul language will no longer trip me up, but I don't count on it. Over time I started having problems with certain kinds of books too, and then came the day when I would have to remove something even more near and dear to me...

One late September day I was hired along with 4 other actors in Seattle to play an interactive role for a private Halloween party. The event planner was a friend who knew me from church, and all 5 of us performers were Believers. *Surely, this family friendly activity would be appropriate for me. I even thought, how cool that God would help me supplement my income with this fun acting opportunity! (Let's just say, Drawing Water was a ministry of great rewards, but most never made it to the bank.)* The party sounded incredible. The hosting clients lived on an estate on Mercer Island and they had thought of everything. There would be different food stations under large tents placed throughout the grounds. A band would be playing in the courtyard and the children's costume contest, pumpkin carving activity, and relay race games were all set to be staged on the sport court. The central feature however, would be a tour through our hosts' mansion, fully decked out as a haunted house. The 5 of us actors—playing a vampire, a witch, a mad scientist, a mummy, and yours truly as a ghost—were to mingle with the guests and interact with them in character. We were asked to prepare back stories (in my case, how I "died"), and to find ways to interact with as many guests as possible within our area of the home. Happily I joined the project and began working on my role. The hosting clients had also arranged for a per diem for each actor for a good costume and make-up, and Tracie (cast as the witch) and I had a ball finding just the right look for our new characters. I had the voice down, the style of movement, a signature laugh, and even a couple of potential death stories, but it all came to a sudden stop. Just two weeks after I was invited to participate in the event and had begun making preparations, I heard it in my spirit—this job was NOT FOR ME. *I'm not casting stones here about other Believers who work on these kinds of special events, or making a generalization about Halloween itself.* However, I had reached a point in my faith walk where **I learned that words have power to positively or negatively impact our thoughts, our health, and our outlook.** This is especially true when we are literally speaking life or death over ourselves. (I'll be talking more about this in the next chapter.) Additionally, in my personal experience, I already knew how spiritual opposition could take full advantage of my heightened visual sensitivity and spin up my thought life. Admittedly, I was honest in my disappointment at having to give up the job when I talked it over with Jesus, but I also knew He was right.

The event planner wasn't happy with me at all, but this was a clear occasion for me to walk my talk, and exercise healthy boundaries. Pleasing God had to trump pleasing man. I turned in my costume, the receipt and unused portion of the per diem, and suggested a good replacement actor whom I knew to be available to the event planner. In turn, he told me that this kind of performing opportunity wouldn't be offered my way again. *Ouch.* And then the most amazing thing happened showing once again how Good our God is, and that He sees our obedience. Within three weeks of my stepping down out of the project, the Haunted House was not only suddenly and surprisingly cancelled by the hosts, but our Drawing Water Christmas performing schedule for that year "miraculously" filled up completely.

Once my identity in Christ was secure, the Holy Spirit began to lead me towards learning more about the anointing and authority we carry with that spiritual identity, and my faith grew exponentially. I know this will be controversial for some of you; unfortunately, many churches do a very poor job of teaching about the Holy Spirit or how we are to operate in the spiritual realm. Yet, as I've already shared in multiple stories, I heard from God in multiple ways from the very beginning of my faith journey. These dreams and visions, inspirations and learnings are REAL. *If the Church doesn't teach about the things of the Spirit, who do you think is going to fill in the void?*

The more I learned in scripture about my identity in Christ, the more I recognized the significance of being called a Royal Priesthood[xix], and the more I studied about the ongoing work of the Holy Spirit and how we can actually partner with Him, the more that I began to ask for Spiritual gifts and mentors to help me activate them. **Indwelled with the Holy Spirit from the time we ask Jesus into our hearts, we have God's power and anointing in our lives. Yet, how many of us ever really learn to walk in it?** The Lord first answered my prayers by bringing me to a Huddle group of Believers committed to Kingdom living. It was an exciting time where, by practicing prophetic activation and seeing in the Spirit (while making sure that everything we were sensing aligned with God's Word), we were all growing in wisdom and discernment. It was in this group that I first learned of the concept of asking God for a thematic Word for my year, and He did not disappoint! That first New Year's Day leading into 2011, Jesus gave me the Word "Freedom," and it was such a powerful teaching tool throughout my year. I wasn't just free <u>from</u>... (shame, insecurities, unhealthy choices); I was free <u>to</u>... (call forth full authority as a child of God—binding/loosing, declaring healing power, asking for complete vision). For the first time I understood what freedom true forgiveness brings, and I was given many "aha" discoveries on the relationship between freedom and PEACE.

In the year the Lord was to teach me about "Abundance," my relationship with Jesus reached a whole new level, and I have been "on fire" to share the fullness of this life ever since! Called to write a blog a couple of years earlier, I was suddenly awakened regularly with inspired messages to post. I wish I could say I delivered them brilliantly or that I knew anything about furthering their reach through social media channels etc., yet today I'm both grateful and humbled by the outpouring in this period. The Holy Spirit was teaching me about so many things I never realized—about how we can be negatively influenced by the spirit of lack, effectively cutting off God's blessings to us! Post after post came flying out of this broken vessel—stories about letting the fear of not having enough pinch off our generosity, stories of letting bitterness and complaint rob us of our joy and wonder, and even stories of financially well-off people focusing on their "poor" circumstances when comparing themselves to those possessing even more. What a waste... True abundance has nothing to do with our stuff; in fact, as I learned, concern over the stuff of life can get in the way of God's blessings!! Not only does our Loving Father want us to enjoy the gifts of answered dreams, but He goes further—fulfilling them beyond our wildest imagination! His Word tells us that He gives us the desires of our heart[xx]. Once you deeply receive the truth of that Promise, you'll never again feel like you don't have "enough."

It was a year where through that Word, "Abundance," given to me by the Holy Spirit, I found great spiritual growth, emotional healing, and in God's goodness, even application in the natural world. Friends and readers encouraged me to put my posts together with related teaching into a workbook, and my first book, <u>Going Deeper-Building an Intimate Walk with the Spirit of God</u> was published in the following year. Additionally, a dream of mine since childhood for travel in Europe was fulfilled.

From beginning to end, this vacation became an incredible illustration of God's perfect timing in answering dreams. Had I ever had the opportunity to travel there earlier, I would have missed so many blessings. Now, just before turning 50, I had a different heart prayer for the trip than I would have held as a younger woman. I prayed for opportunities to meet real people in authentic, non-touristy situations, and Abba answered this request again and again. On planes and trains, in cafes, shops, and museums, I enjoyed several wonderful conversations with regular people about their daily lives— their hopes and their challenges. Though we often had to work to understand each other given the language barriers, (me with French last used in high school and a Rosetta Stone course in Italian) I found people were genuinely appreciative of my efforts to get to know them. Whether talking about traditions with a gondolier whose father, grandfather, and great-grandfather were also all gondoliers, or talking to a retired teacher from Italy about her new life in Paris and listening to her struggles making friends with the locals, or talking to an octogenarian Parisian gentleman about how his city had changed, and what has remained the same—I felt so honored that they would so graciously share their stories with me. Starting these conversations was awkward for me, but as it turned out, these people wanted to be known as much as I wanted to know them! I've thought about this quite a bit ever since. And in the years that followed, the Lord Has shown me time and again that this gift of really seeing and affirming the people we come in contact with within our daily lives is one of the most powerful blessings we can ever experience.

Another year in which a thematic Word so richly deepened my faith walk was 2018—the year in which I was to learn about God's "Glory." I know I've already mentioned how the Holy Spirit began teaching me and my emotional response from the very beginning of that year, but there is a very important story addition from my time learning more about the Lord's Presence that I have to share:

I had a day that I will forever describe as my "Awe Day," but it didn't start out that way. While I drove to Seattle that morning for my regular shift as a volunteer at the Washington Talking Book and Braille Library, I was feeling kind of blah. I don't remember having a particularly bad morning, it was just gray and quiet, and I hadn't fully adjusted yet to life without a regular, or even part-time job. Worship music was playing in the car as I crossed the bridge and drove into the city, and I'm sure on some heart level that helped, but at the time my focus was on the running check list in my head. You know the one—*After my shift in the studio I need to stop by the grocery store, figure out dinner, walk the dog, do the laundry...* The drive wasn't memorable in the least. The sky was gray and cloudy, pretty typical for that time of the year. There was the usual amount of traffic, and the usual scary left turn from a "suicide lane" to a small adjacent street—directly in front of cars climbing a steep hill on a blind approach. Still, I made it safely into the library parking lot, signed in for admittance, and prepared to begin recording in the sound studio I reserved. Sound levels were checked and I had just begun my recording when the pounding began. Some renovations were being done to an office upstairs and unfortunately, the usual sound proofing in a recording studio simply couldn't silence this level of construction noise. I waited for a little while, trying to record in the short 3-5 minute pauses from the upstairs pounding that would occur every few minutes, but finally I decided to end my session. Admittedly I was frustrated. I smiled as I waved goodbye to the staff member who had helped me set my recording levels, but inwardly I was pretty whiny. *I wish someone had notified me that the construction upstairs was going on today. I'll probably have to re-record everything I attempted, and then there's the gas and the tolls, and almost getting clipped on that stupid left turn!* Aren't you glad God doesn't smack us like we deserve every time we get whiny? Instead on this day, Abba chose to overwhelm me with Awe.

I was heading back across the floating bridge when it began. It was as though everything released at once. The sun burst out from behind the clouds, its light sparkling off the surface of the lake on either side of the bridge. The chorus of one of my favorite worship songs came to a swell and I couldn't stop myself from belting out, "I'm a child of God, Yes I am!"[xxi] And in His amazing goodness, Jesus flooded my mind and heart with wave after wave of reminders of how and when He had been there for me in my past. Times of healing and restoration, gifts of provision and purpose, the divine appointments and God kisses and miraculous ways in which He has demonstrated His love for me through the years—Are you getting this? This moment driving home wasn't a new visitation. With nothing more than the activation of precious memories I felt His presence so fully, so richly, I was completely undone. I cried and cried, joyful tears this time as the realization hit home. **NEXT to God, with His majesty, His beauty and power and love and goodness, we are <u>nothing</u>, and yet TO God, we are <u>everything</u>!** To this day, even the act of just writing down this truth takes my breath away. Have you taken this in for yourself? You are CHERISHED BEYOND MEASURE by the Creator of the Universe!

On a side note: Given what I've been sharing throughout this book about weeping with the Lord, it might surprise you to know that for years I barely cried at all. My feelings were stuffed deep down and bottled up tight; I only allowed my tears for appropriate dramatic performances. In fact, people who I had invited to my plays would frequently comment, "I always knew you'd make me laugh, but I never knew you'd make me cry." Good emotional health is one of the blessed benefits of living the Abundant life Jesus wants us to enjoy.

I began this chapter by talking about how we have to truly WANT an intimate relationship with Jesus to experience the abundant life of Joy and Peace He provides. *You don't have to wait until heaven before your eternal promises begin!* Are you seeking and recognizing His Presence with you daily? If I can share one tool that has forever changed the consistency (and therefore growth) in my faith walk—let me encourage you to begin keeping a journal as part of your Quiet Time. There's a reason God's Word tells His children to REMEMBER over and over; the truth is, we're a very forgetful bunch. Yet when you journal, when you can see the evidence of how your thinking has changed, how the Lord has been with you through all of the ups and downs, and how rich your life has become, it fortifies you for the road ahead. If you're already thinking, "no, nope, nada, not gonna happen," STOP and hear me out… I didn't think I could do it either. Memories of "Dear Diary" entries from 7-year-old me, or later 11-year-old me, or still later 13-year-old me—all 5 or 6 entries before I'd quit—kept me from even considering keeping a faith journal. And then some friends in a Bible study talked about an approach of using a journal to help engage with God in a two-way conversation. A lightbulb went on for me and I've talked with Him, asked questions, reflected on scripture, dreams, and worship song lyrics regularly since January 2009. In that same time frame He has encouraged me, guided me, convicted me of error, forgiven me, and overall—met me in ways I never imagined possible, this side of heaven. It's a personal relationship that has quite literally transformed my life from the inside out.

In the opening chapter I shared a little bit about being healed of the emotional wounds I carried since childhood. Although today I am truly, thankfully free of agreements that "odd," or "unworthy" are a part of who I am, I will occasionally notice that indeed I continue to be the *unique* woman God designed me to be. Perhaps in part to my personality –which admittedly can get pretty intense when I get excited about something, perhaps in part because of my secular upbringing, or perhaps because of my artistic sensibilities and different ways of seeing the world, I am not what you might think of when you imagine a Bible studying church lady. *Through the years I have been enormously grateful for the graciousness of the women who not only have lived their whole lives within the church, but who have still managed to encourage rather than condemn me for my discussion questions and unusual perspective.* However, I cannot tell you what joy it brought me through the experience of journaling and seeing for myself how our Heavenly Father is a God of patterns, that (despite what is often seen in the present) I could finally fully believe He has plans for all kinds of unique creative types to make meaningful contributions to the Church. Did you ever read about how God supernaturally gifted artists to work on His tabernacle in the wilderness? "And Moses told them, 'The Lord has filled Bezalel with the Spirit of God, giving him great wisdom, intelligence and skill in all kinds of crafts. He is able to create beautiful objects from gold, silver, and bronze. He is skilled in cutting and setting gemstones and in carving wood. In fact, he has every necessary skill. And the Lord has given both him and Oholiab son of Ahisamach, of the tribe of Dan, the ability to teach their skills to others.'"(Ex 35:31-34 NLT)

Or what about Michelangelo? According to history, while Michelangelo did have some faith struggles, he was a devoted believer in Jesus; for him, the commission from the Pope to paint the ceiling of the Sistine Chapel wasn't just about the money. For four years, Michelangelo sacrificially poured himself into this work. He built special scaffolding and while he didn't actually paint lying on his back as some stories suggest, he did suffer for years from standing, crouching, bending backwards, etc., forcing his body to endure the pain necessary to complete this work. Add to this, the whole time he painted he agonized over doubts of his abilities and worthiness; Michelangelo considered himself a sculptor, not a painter at all. I can only imagine the comfort the Lord gave him, perhaps showing him in visions what the hands of God and Adam might look like, perhaps whispering in his spirit—"atta boy, Mikey." *From my own experiences writing Drawing Water scripts that profoundly shared God's truths before I knew them myself, I know that the Holy Spirit does the same thing for His artists today!* Made in the image of God, it makes perfect sense that God's people would be artists! The medium may be music, clay, metal working, comedy, baking, fashion, computer software, architecture, and so on, but we all inherit the longing to create. Through the centuries some forms of artistic expression have been embraced by the church and then alternatively discarded because they were deemed too "worldly." Well of course! The enemy is known for counterfeiting the things of God—especially those things that can draw others to Jesus! *A note for those of you who may be involved in church leadership: in a year when some lawmakers deemed worship gatherings as unessential, can you relate to the heart of your artists who grieve when you banish or limit the arts in your churches? Many of today's artists are gifted prophetically; imagine how they could serve alongside to glorify God and edify His people!*

My entire life changed for the better once I understood how God truly sees me and how He has gifted me with purpose so that I can contribute meaningfully to His Kingdom. Along the way I've learned so much, not the least of which was to live in forgiveness without regret, and humility without shame.

So how about You? Are you using your spiritual gifts? Have you figured out how you hear best from the Lord? One of my favorite Christian lifestyle books that helped me build a consistent discipline for meeting with Jesus is Gary Thomas' <u>Sacred Pathways</u>[xxii]. The truth of the matter is, I am not good at doing the same thing, the same way, over, and over, and over again. I thrive on variety, and so when I learned that "Quiet Time" didn't mean I had to get up each morning before daylight with my Bible and my prayer list, that I actually might hear best from God outside on a hike… or sharing about Him with others… or by singing to worship music… it opened the door for me to make our relationship uniquely personal. Over the years I've made a prayer closet, created an online Kingdom Living group, worshipped as I've walked my dog, and lit candles—practicing lectio divina (slow scripture reading with contemplation and prayer to engage with God.) If you've never found a consistent meeting that works for you, I encourage you to experiment too! **The full, abundant life Jesus wants us to have can only happen through daily connection with the lover of your soul.** I guarantee, if you lean in and try, He will meet you and teach you as you go!!

CHAPTER 7

Prepared for Battle

For we are not fighting against flesh-and-blood enemies, but against evil rulers and authorities of the unseen world, against mighty powers in this dark world, and against evil spirits in the heavenly places. (Eph 6:12 NLT)

I live in an older home with hardwood floors, and though I don't fully understand the science of why wood expands and contracts with moisture and temperature, I can see the effects. In the last several nights when the overnight temperature has dipped into the low 30's, I have placed a large rolled up towel under the back door to help keep the frigid air from creeping in under the door. In winter we can all feel what happens when we're not careful to seal the cracks and the chinks in the natural realm. *Yet how many of us are as careful to guard possible cracks or chinks in the spiritual realm?*

The other night I started watching "Married at First Sight" on Netflix. Now this isn't a show that I'm recommending, it's just that that night, I had reached my fill of Hallmark Christmas movies and finished the latest season of the British Baking Show; I had also already viewed the interview being broadcast on my new go-to T.V. station, TBN, and I just wanted something to keep me company until bedtime. While this particular Netflix reality-based, relationship-finding style television show wasn't as awful (imagery wise) as others I've seen and quickly dismissed, the problem was, as soon as the first episode ended, the second began and there I sat like a lump watching the first 3 episodes in a row. *Would the four couples all go through with it and marry perfect strangers? Did it look like they were connecting, that the marriages may actually be successful in the long run? How were their friends and families responding to all of this? Was God present in any of it?* By the time the third episode wrapped up, it was time for bed. And then it started. My mind thought about those eight people all night long. I realized I had wasted brain space and thought life, but now I was embarrassed, hiding from Jesus. After all, I was the one who opened the door to something I knew could be a problem for me—binge watching anything typically does this. What right did I have to come to Jesus for peace now? *(You can hear the lie, right? How quickly and easily the enemy can sneak in, even with mature believers!)*

Early the next morning I repented of my choices and talked to Jesus at length about how sorry I was for opening this door—or at the very least, not sealing up the crack under it—allowing myself to be influenced in ways I knew weren't good for me. Then I turned on worship music: "And all my life You have been faithful. And all my life You have been so, so good. With every breath that I am able, oh I will sing of the goodness of God!"[xxiii] *SERIOUSLY?* Once again the Lord gave me exactly what I needed; now crying and grateful I knew, I was free to start fresh. I asked Abba to let me be a blessing to others, whether during that day's errands or in something I could share as I continued writing this for You. **This chapter is important because the more you follow the Lord, seeking to live out the abundant life of Joy and Peace He promises, the more the enemy will bring all kinds of spiritual warfare against you.** Some of it, you'll bring on yourself. If like me, you catch yourself practicing "cheap grace" (knowing things that lead you into sinful behaviors or attitudes and choosing to do them anyway) turn away from them immediately (the Bible calls this, "Repenting"), and trust in Him and His goodness to faithfully help you correct your course. Don't make the mistake of so many others by beating yourself up over and over again with your weaknesses and failures. *Do you BELIEVE you're truly forgiven?* Keep your focus on HIM—without wallowing in you—and these sinful habits or behaviors will dramatically decrease in frequency and intensity.

While spiritual opposition comes against EVERY believer, we don't always recognize these attacks for what they are. It wasn't until Tracie and I started Drawing Water Ministry that I began to realize exactly how sneaky and how relentless the demonic world can be in attempting to pull us out of commission. *If the enemy can get us distracted or worse yet, if he can get us to agree with him, he can win the little battles. The good news is that all we have to do for total victory is to stand. With God, the war is already won!*

What follows are some examples of spiritual attacks that came against Drawing Water, but I assure you, since learning to recognize opposition for what it is, I have also seen all of these come against me in my regular (non-ministry) life ever since.

We began to notice that physical ailments and illnesses started popping up out of the blue, especially on ministry days. Sore muscles, cysts, sinus headaches, laryngitis, food poisoning… all kinds of things seemed to try to wiggle their way in in an attempt to get us to abandon our calling. Once there was a season of fibromyalgia symptoms, and frequently we performed in spite of chronic pain. While in no way am I suggesting that these kinds of things aren't really happening or aren't to be taken seriously, I do strongly recommend turning to our ultimate Healer before checking in at the local medical clinic. For us, it was incredibly affirming to note how God would supernaturally hold back physical limitations brought on by aches, pains, and even dizziness or nausea as soon as our programs began. Also notably, by the conclusion of these same programs, not only did the earlier physical symptoms weaken—if they returned at all—but we felt better, stronger, and certainly more confident in the goodness of our faithful Heavenly Father.

Another area of attack came against our calling as the enemy tried to get us to question our worthiness—especially when we were trying new things. I've already mentioned the struggles we had with a certain base commander in our efforts to present Courageous One for the women involved in military life. Would it surprise you to know we also occasionally had conflict with women's ministry team leaders? Through our fourteen years in ministry I can count these occasions on one hand, but nevertheless they were unsettling.

I remember once a woman host sent back my descriptions of the content we would be performing with the note that "a fun, upbeat scene in which two scripture-citing cheerleaders encourage refreshment" sounded a little too "Churchy." Instead, she wanted her event to be more true to life, with real problems brought out into the light. So, per her instructions, we removed the cheerleading scene from the line up and added a more dramatic scene that touched on divorce and loneliness. When the day of the event arrived, we were surprised to see that this woman's tea—-described as an event for bringing out real world issues of life—was decorated in a very prim and proper high tea style, down to the sugar cubes hand painted with frosting flowers. Nevertheless, we performed the program that was requested. The day was actually divided into two seatings with two identical presentations planned. However, after the morning's performance, we were summoned to the women's ministry office where the leader/our hostess basically blasted our choice of performing a scene which included a lonely divorced character. Angrily she informed us that the selection was entirely inappropriate for a spring tea. Never mind that it hadn't been in our original planning until we were prompted to provide something deeper; never mind that dozens of women uncharacteristically stopped us in the hallway to share how grateful they were that we actually shared something thoughtful in a church virtually closed off to helping their people with "taboo topics" of relatable hardships. We felt like we had failed miserably when the women's leader chastised us and demanded we remove the scene from the afternoon's presentation. To say that it was difficult to drum up the courage to go back and perform at the church again that afternoon is an understatement. Now I can laugh at the memory, but at that time... Once again, however, God was really good to us. After the second presentation, the same leader—having since talked to many of her team during the break between seatings—apologized to us, admitting that maybe she hadn't communicated well, and that maybe our presentation was actually more appropriate than she first realized.

Unfortunately, as we discovered, another common tactic of the enemy is to attack family members, or to cause division within our relationships. If he can't get you to feel too sick or tired to keep going, if he can't get you to quit because of doubts or fears about your abilities, he will go after your loved ones. While I was still a fairly young Christian, before Drawing Water and before I knew anything about spiritual opposition, something happened that woke me up to this startling new possibility. I was performing in a large Christmas event at church when my "baby"—then six-years-old— was looking back at his Daddy and older brother as he ran ahead down the church hallway, and then turned forward just in time to smash face first into the corner of a pillar. Yes, the impact split his forehead open and yes, it required stitches. Tim had an usher find me backstage where the performance team was taking a small break before the next service was to begin. I'm sure those of you who are parents can imagine my emotions as after meeting up with Tim and the boys, and giving comfort to both our injured younger son, and our older son—near faint from seeing the cut, we decided that Tim would take the boys to the ER and I would stay for the second performance. Evan had long since stopped crying and true to his character, he was telling me the story of what happened with plenty of gusto. Tim was urging me to stay, and I agreed, knowing I would feel guilty either way. With a major speaking role, no understudy, and an expected crowd of nearly 2000 people coming, to spoil even a portion of this long-awaited ministry outreach event over this minor accident wouldn't be right. Once again though, God was so good to our family! The choir, orchestra, actors, pastors, and entire production team all stopped and prayed for Evan. Then a little while later, as the orchestra played the overture, I received the good news in a message from my husband—"5 stitches, no concussion, Evan has a new teddy bear and is excited to have a scar 'like Harry Potter.'"

Through the years of touring with Drawing Water, many prayers helped us through relationship upsets that directly proceeded or followed ministry events. Arguments with spouses…bickering children calling in tears who wanted mom *to come home now!*... even an occasional disagreement on site would suddenly spring up between Tracie and me, or with one of our other associates on the shelter tours. Given the oily nature of a very real enemy, it wasn't surprising that these attacks would happen—especially leading up to an event in which hearts and lives would be changed, or on the heels of such a victory—but they still would catch us off guard. *Have you ever suddenly found yourself in a heated/emotional argument with your husband or wife over some simple question or comment and wondered, "where did that anger come from?" The enemy's whole game plan is to divide and conquer; don't give him the satisfaction of seeing you fight! When it's happened to us, Tim and I slow down and take a breath—recognizing the opposition for what it is—and we also discover the "hurtful" question or comment was a simple misunderstanding. We've been happily married for over 31 years in part because we are both quick to apologize, forgive, let go, and move forward.*

In addition to personal and relational attacks, Spiritual opposition can also take the form of a disruption to the way things are supposed to operate. We've all experienced this in a year of shutdowns, shelter ins, closures, and LOSS but how many of us chalked this up to the natural world only, and didn't look at the bigger battle in the spiritual realm? *Do you have peace? Are you making decisions out of faith or fear?* In Drawing Water, we came to believe that the greater the opposition, the more that God would be using that particular event, and so we continued on joyfully despite anything and everything that came our way during performances. Funny incidents include: the house dog (golden lab mix) at a women's shelter becoming part of the act when he decided he wanted to keep licking my hand during a musical number, the sound operator at a large Canadian conference who literally missed every one of our sound cues during our 3 performance sets (the audience grew to love "Harold" as we smiled sweetly from around our privacy screen to call out, "not yet Harold," or "it's the next track, Harold."), and the number of times one of our mics would go out or develop a weird growly reverberation (we called it the Satan voice), and Tracie and I would keep performing—awkwardly keeping our heads next to each other to share a mic until we could get a substitute 2nd mic from the sound crew. Anything can happen during a live performance anyway, and when you tour—relying on different equipment and the abilities of strangers in the sound booth, etc.—anything does. Add to this presenting a ministry message and let's just say, it was an education I'll never forget.

However, in fourteen years of ministry together, while there was much that could go wrong, we could count on making a favorable impression on our audiences. We loved the people we served and they loved us back. However, a Biblical truth came alive for me in a very unexpected way at our first Courageous One performance—presented at a naval air station in western Washington. While our intent and material were all very clear from the onset for these free performances for the women in military life, we shared about "God," our "faith," the "Bible," and our own testimonies freely, but chose to minimize our mention of Jesus Himself in these secular settings. Through the course of the program as the women grew to trust us and see that we weren't going to be preaching at them or judging them, we would talk more about services on base where they could find "prayer" support or confidential "Christian" counseling. All was going well during the presentation UNTIL... I shared the Bible story about the men who lowered their friend on a cot through a roof, believing that "Jesus" could heal him.[xxiv] No sooner did I say the name of Jesus when a woman stood up from nearly the back row of what was essentially a set of bleachers, to literally—and with great fanfare—march down through the center aisle of the audience. Stomp, stomp, stomp… the bleachers rattled with each step, and I… well…, I just kept sharing the story, making connections to their lives and our program theme, ("You are not alone"). Eventually, the woman made it down to the front riser where she marched off, perhaps frustrated that I didn't stop to challenge her or beg her to stay, and then she left the auditorium with a clang of the heavy metal door. I wondered how the audience would react to her departure, but they simply kept their focus on me, several of them caught up in the story by this time, and actually leaning forward and nodding with understanding. **Never forget, when you stand with the Lord, you've already won.**

Earlier I mentioned how sometimes we can actually inadvertently open the door for demonic activity and I would be doing you a disservice if I didn't take the time here to more thoroughly share about the power we wield with our words. In Drawing Water Ministry, I found myself at one point "agreeing with the enemy" when I would share about the many previous difficulties we had had with sound as we were setting up for each new event. Tracie alerted me to my growing habit of warning the tech crew on site of the kinds of misfortunes that would probably occur and I apologized, admitting she was right. There was no reason to expect trouble with our microphones or the sound cues and yet my regular use of talking about these former difficulties gave them new strength. **We are Spirit beings, formed in the image of our Creator God who spoke creation into being. Doesn't it make sense that even in our day to day, non-ministry life, we could be speaking life or death with our words all the time?** The Book of James cautions Believers about the power of the tongue[xxv], and in my own life I have very specific examples of both the ability to build/bring life and the power to destroy/bring death found in our words.

When Tim and I first married, though we both had some woundedness and resulting co-dependency that would eventually need healing, we also developed a beautiful arrangement right away: Though he left for work each morning well before dawn, he'd kiss me goodbye and we'd sleepily tell one another, "I love you." When he came home from work, he often would need a little time to decompress from his day before he could positively engage in conversation or family news of the day, but we told each other "I love you" before he retreated into our home office for about 30 minutes. At night regardless of what time either of us would go to bed, we always told each other, "I love you." Over the years this routine has remained in place, and both of us would tell you, without a doubt it has contributed to the glue that has seen us through. In every relationship there can be ups and downs and a good marriage takes work from both partners. However, even in times where we've argued, even in times where we may have felt a little more distant from one another, even in times of hectic business travel or outside family pressures, even in a year of physical separation due in part to the season of Covid, I have never for an instant been uncertain of his love for me. *Friends, if you can have this steadfast faithfulness with a person, someone as full of faults as you, imagine what you can have with the Lover of your soul when you take the time to talk with Him daily!*

Where Tim and I built life into our relationship with our words, sadly, my mother did the opposite. She lost both of her parents to cancer when she was in her early 30's and they were both in their early 60's. Next she lost both her older brother and older sister to cancer when each of them reached around 60 years of age. It didn't matter to my mother that all of these immediate relatives were smokers and she was not, she just began confessing that she would "be gone by 60." While I didn't understand this at the time, now I can see how she literally willed death into being by the power of her speech and the beliefs they etched into her Spirit. My mother was diagnosed with Alzheimer's at age 60, and she passed away a few weeks before her 68th birthday. Today I'm sensitive to people, women especially, who will start down-playing themselves or making unflattering comments about their age, their attractiveness, their abilities, or their worth. The enemy loves to whisper lies to us, but we don't have to listen or agree with him! The abundant life that Jesus came to give us builds us up to see beauty and joy and peace and love. Anything less than that doesn't deserve our attention.

We also allow spiritual opposition to darken our thoughts when we stop being present in our own lives in favor of watching and comparing ourselves to others. This can happen so subtly over time… Have you ever visited a social media site for a quick check in only to discover later that you've wasted over an hour scrolling through various posts and photos of people you barely know? Have you ever noticed how many people seated in restaurants are more glued to their cell phones than connected to their dining partners in conversation? God's PRESENCE is in the present. We can miss Him by our own volition!

I'll never forget the gondola ride Tim and I scheduled with our tour guide in the year we were blessed with a family vacation in Italy…

It was a warm, beautiful evening in Venice, with lantern lights bouncing off the canal waters, and an eager collection of tourists piling into the five boats reserved for our group. Our gondolier arranged the seating of our 6-person party for balance. (At 6'3", my husband Tim was chosen to sit in the bow facing inwards while I was placed near him, but not next to him.) Once we got under way, I understood. Gliding along narrow channels and under low bridges, the gondolier was like a ballet dancer—gracefully extending his leg to gently push us off a wall, or arching his body in another direction to move us along with the rowing oar. At one point, the husband partner of the couple in the middle of the boat, asked Tim to lean to the side so that he could snap a picture, and the gondolier immediately gave Tim a heated warning for nearly knocking him off his perch from the gondola's stern. Fortunately for my husband and me, it was but a tiny blip in a perfect evening. Unfortunately for the husband and wife in the center of the boat, their frustrations had just begun. Gracefully the five gondolas slid on top of the water toward the Grand Canal, passing semi-submerged homes with people out on their verandahs, and under beautifully arched bridgeways. It was so romantic! The husband with the camera continued to complain that the aperture wouldn't open enough to compensate for the low light. Then the five boats reached the Grand Canal where they positioned themselves side by side for a musical serenade. The gondolier in the center boat sang an incredible rendition of Santa Lucia as the gondolier to his left softly played a guitar. Honestly, I'm weeping again now just thinking of it. Tim and I shared long looks and whispered loving words; although we couldn't quite reach each other to hold hands, we were both so grateful to God for this incredible, beautiful gift. The man with the camera and his unhappy wife bickered with one another about keeping the camera steady while the boats gently rocked in the water. That poor couple were so focused on getting the perfect picture they completely lost sight of the fact that they were on a romantic gondola ride on a glorious moonlit night. **When taken to the extreme, capturing images of living abundantly can actually rob you of experiencing it!**

One thing that I never expected is the amount of spiritual opposition that will come at you from those who should be on your side. As I've mentioned, I began my faith journey later than many people do. I didn't grow up going to church, and I never realized that the same problems that exist in the outside world exist within the body of Believers. God's people are broken, messy, and just as prone to the temptations of sin as anyone else. Unfortunately, the devil does some of his best work from within the Church itself. I once attended a service in a "Christian" church in which two members read long passages of scripture without any explanation given and then the minister gave a sermon about an upcoming international fair and "how all roads lead to heaven." I also once visited a church service in which the pastor basically condemned all of the fathers in the room with the pronouncement that it was completely their fault if their children had any problems in life—*the sins of the father.* At a time perhaps more crucial than any time before in history, the Church (capital "C", God's body of Believers, not a building) needs to stand up for the full canon of scripture; we need to speak the whole truth in Love. This is not the time for pride, fear, political correctness, or any other watered-down version of who Jesus is. The old models have to go.

While I'm on the subject, I'm going to stick my neck out here with the observations of one who has lived both as a Christ follower in a non-Christian friendly culture, and now in the Bible belt. This may surprise some of you but those of you who grew up where you can talk easily about Jesus in any gathering, and where crosses and decorative scripture items are sold alongside clothing in popular shops, could learn a few things from those who have to work harder and under greater adversity to remain a committed follower. Hear me on this one, I know there are many wonderful, loving, godly people in the south who walk the walk with maturity and grace. However, there is also a Religious spirit that has been allowed to infiltrate among you as can happen with any body of believers who've been in the trenches for a long time—*the Pharisees and the Prodigal Son's older brother come to mind.*xxvi From my experience, when a person in the Pacific Northwest chooses to make the study of God's Word a priority in their life, they rarely if ever miss a Bible study class that they've gone to the trouble of joining. Think about it: If people in your workplace are going to challenge your beliefs and make fun of your faith, wouldn't you want to be certain of who God is and what He says? On the other hand, I've noticed that some participants in Bible study classes in the south don't seem too concerned about missing one or several of the classes in a series; *after all they've known Jesus since childhood.* Remember, one day in the near future the opportunity to study God's Word may not be so readily available.

Also, those who are serious about following the Lord in an area like Seattle—and again, while in a culture that is highly suspect of faith if not against it—will tend to be more open and real about their challenges/prayer needs as well as their successes/praises. Similar vulnerability can be far too risky among southerners influenced by the Religious spirit. Recently while attending a women's Bible study in Texas, a woman in the class suddenly looked at me during our discussion and bravely stated that she would "never have it together" like I did. Recognizing the lie she was listening to, I immediately encouraged her by sharing one of the struggles I had been dealing with just two days earlier *(emotional eating-stuffing my feelings)*. In a faith community surrounded by those unfriendly to the faith such as in the Seattle area, that's what you do. You love with compassion. You are willing to humble yourself and admit your own sins and weaknesses for the good of the whole. You share truth and forgiveness and God's strength to try again another day. Imagine my surprise when one of my new Southern sisters—with a smile plastered on her face—called me a glutton. Then to make sure I was appropriately shamed and put in my place, she went on to share how gluttony was just as big a sin as any other. *Brothers and Sisters in Christ, is that what you call speaking truth in Love? Honestly, if I had been a baby in the faith I would have run away and never come back to church again.*

Please hear my heart on this one. On this side of heaven, while we are still formed of broken human nature, we are sinful people. Paul admitted to as much. "For I know that nothing good lives within the flesh of my fallen humanity. The longings to do what is right are within me, but will-power is not enough to accomplish it. My lofty desires to do what is good are dashed when I do the things I want to avoid." (Rom 7:18-19 TPT) This is our reality, but by the grace of Jesus, it is not our destiny. It would be foolish to blame all of our failures on spiritual opposition—*the devil made me do it.* For the last several years during this long transitional season, Abba has been teaching me to look at my sinful habits, to find the doors I leave cracked open, to repent immediately and fully for my part and for the part of all of humanity in what we have made of His beautiful creation. I would never tell you that 'I have it all together' in my faith walk; in fact the more I mature, the more I recognize how far I have yet to go to be the woman God has called me to be. But we're

not to live in shame and guilt and hopelessness over these things—
THAT is the enemy's voice. Instead, I have learned to look at these
moments as wonderfully humbling learning opportunities. Abba is
slowly but surely sandpapering off my rough spots. Repentance isn't
about shame at all, but a gift that He uses to refine us for His Glory.

I know that I've already written about the importance of Bible
study, Quiet time with God, and the value of connecting and learning
with other faithful people. These all lead to the abundant rich life with
Jesus that this whole book is meant to convey. However, we can't ignore
the first part of our foundational scripture from John 10:10 which says,
"the thief is only there to steal, kill, and destroy" (MSG) Friends, we
are living in times when the enemy is working overtime to ruin God's
children in every conceivable way. If you have never really thought about
spiritual battle preparation, I encourage you to start now! Ask the Holy
Spirit for guidance. He is With you and For you. Two specific strategies
have really helped me. When I know I am heading into a battle, or
suspect one coming, or can see the effects of it around me, I immediately
start focusing on the armor of God.[xxvii] (Eph 6:11-18) Every piece of it
is important. In my mind's eye, I envision Jesus helping me on with my
breastplate and my helmet. I make sure my boots are securely fashioned
so that I can stand. And my shield? Well, it's large enough to help cover
those around me who are frightened. I also gain strength in battle
preparation through worship and praise. "First it was Fragrance… Then
it Turned to Fire… My Worship is my Weapon…This is how I Win my
Battle"[xviii] Whether you most relate to the old hymns or something more
contemporary, find your anthem song—something you can sing from
your heart at a moment's notice and that fills you with joy, reminding
you of the One who is on your side.

Finally, TRUST… When the going gets really tough, when
everything looks impossible, get ready to watch your Heavenly
Father work on your behalf![xxix]

*What follows is a true story—recaptured here from my blog, posted
in January 2020.[xxx] May it bless you as the memory blesses our family.*

In early December of 2019 my younger son and I headed out onto the road with a mini U-Haul trailer hitched to his 19 year old car, in order to move him the approximately 2,000 miles from the Pacific Northwest to northern Texas. Winter weather had already blasted through much of the country, and more storms were expected. To be honest, this was not a drive I looked forward to. We considered different routes, evaluating the hazards of mountain passes or driving through punishing rain. I also knew it would take us several days because I didn't want to drive after dark when I wouldn't see as well or have as much reaction time. (Don't forget we were pulling a trailer!) I am grateful for the family and friends who prayed for us, for my brother—an experienced truck driver who gave us sound advice and the safest route possible, and for my husband—who hurriedly helped us pack to leave earlier than we originally planned to get ahead of the worst of the expected storms. **However, this road trip will be forever remembered with gratitude for the obvious work of protecting angels who on numerous occasions, moved us safely out of danger.** One day it was a driver who pulled out quickly from where she had been stopped by a police officer on the left side of a four lane, 70-mile-an-hour freeway; inexplicably she raced across three of the four lanes landing in front of us, and then she slowed to a stop. *On the freeway.* Again, I was pulling a trailer! Miraculously, and with all praise to Abba—we avoided colliding with her. Another day a herd of what looked like baby elk came running in a circular pattern directly toward the freeway and then just as suddenly, turned their course instead to run parallel to it, alongside the right-side lane, against the traffic. (We were in the right lane, where we became oh so relieved that they didn't turn their parade directly into our car!)

And then there was the day we drove over Elk Mountain (I-80 in Wyoming). The signs posted warned of some wind gusts and slick spots, but we were advised that if we proceeded carefully we would be fine. The highway cameras showed sunshine dawning and clear open roads. Later as we approached the peak, we found white-out conditions as wind gusts blew snow from a previous storm in great billows across the road. Visibility became really limited and at one point heading down hill, I stepped on my brake to slow us down further, and that's when it happened: We hit black ice and began sliding down the road with the trailer whipping around from behind us first to the left, then to the right. It was terrifying! I clearly had no control of the car, and we began spinning around on the freeway. "Help us, God!" I cried out, and **He was right there.** When we came to a stop we were off the road, on the shoulder, facing the WRONG WAY. We were shaken up to be sure, but we didn't receive a bruise, a scratch to the car, or any other impairment. Miraculously no one else came careening into us, pushing us off the mountain, and Divinely, a highway patrol officer was on the scene within seconds of our spin out. When I look back at it, I can laugh with wonder, but that day it was more about the kind of nervous laughter that comes up with sheer terror. The officer, unable to get us turned around to head in the right direction on the freeway, guided us up the shoulder for about a mile– He went backwards in his police car; we followed closely behind the nose of his car. Then he got back out of his car and though practically blinded by the gusting wind, he managed to direct us into the emergency access lane that goes between the north and south (or was it east and west?) directions of a freeway, and we headed back up the hill, only to get off at the first exit, turn around, and start all over again!!!

This time, after we had turned around and headed back once more in the original direction, I had my hazard lights on and I allowed myself to go no faster than 30 miles an hour. And do you know not one car or truck ventured to pass us until we were well down the mountain? My son kept his eyes peeled to the side of the road for the white line painted there–the only thing we could see that kept us on the lane for sure, and the time I felt what was undoubtedly another icy patch, we were going so slow we just coasted for a second through it. The whole way down the mountain I verbally thanked and praised our Father for taking such good care of us. And by the time we were safely at the bottom, my son also knew in his own heart how God Himself rescued us that day!

CLOSING

Your Turn

For God has not given us a spirit of fear and timidity, but of power, love, and self-discipline. So never be ashamed to tell others about our Lord. (2 Tim 1:7-8 NLT)

As I've walked with Jesus for a number of years now I can see that He is not only with me IN difficult seasons or during circumstances that in the past would have shaken me to the core and knocked me off my feet, but He actually prepares me for them in ADVANCE. Now in wrapping up this little book of stories I am prompted to ask you to consider something: *Is it possible that He drew you to read along with me in order that He might open your eyes in a new way, preparing You too?*

A few years ago I was given a very memorable dream. This dream felt like a profound warning to me—it was so detailed and complete. Further along on my Spiritual walk, I wondered if I was supposed to share this somehow? Yet, not having been called into the Office of Prophet by God, I didn't know what a regular lay person is supposed to do with this kind of message. What kind of prophetic visions and dreams are to be shared? And when? And how? I told my women's ministry leader and a couple of trusted Christian friends about it and they all also saw how this relates to End Times prophetic warnings in the Bible[xxxi], but none of them had much experience with dreams. One of them suggested I meet with her friend, a Christian mentor who could talk about dreams with me, and the two of us met monthly for my last few years in Seattle.

While I could see and understand how this dream has pointed to our culture ever since I first experienced it, this is the time that Abba was pointing to. When I finally stopped allowing myself to get caught up and influenced by the conversation of pandemics and politics and protests on everyone's lips, Jesus reminded me of this dream with such urgency that it prompted me to write this book.

When the dream began I was standing at a table at a ministry fair event and one of the pastors from my church sat on the other side. (This wasn't one of the pastors I had a relationship with, but he knew who I was, and from the occasional times he gave the message during the Sunday service, I knew he had a real heart for God.) Pastor Marty leaned forward with his usual big smile on his face, "Have you seen the Sky Mirror?" I hadn't. Immediately the scene changed and I was overlooking this beautiful, bucolic outdoor space. Rolling hills, grassy green lawns, a sparkling blue stream with a large wooden pedestrian bridge arched over it… it was perfect! I could feel a gentle breeze, see butterflies on swaying flower tops, and the colors were brighter, more distinct—blues, greens, yellows, reds—than I had ever seen. Once I adjusted to the environment, I began to see the people. Going and coming, professionally dressed and casually clothed in jeans, men and women, young adults and aging seniors, people of different ethnicities, races, body types, and economic status, these were representatives of ALL kinds of people in our world. The thing that was most noticeable, however, is that each of these people were moving through this beautiful scene within their own clear plastic ball. They looked like hamster balls, or those big, human-sized rolling, or floating balls you can climb into at some fairs.

A woman appeared at my side and she explained, "They don't know they're in the balls. They think they're seeing the world clearly."

I remember feeling sad for them. The people seemed to be happy and productive but they were missing out on the extraordinary beauty and freedom outside the balls. Then something changed and the plastic-looking balls or globes stopped moving. Suspended in motion, my eyes could focus better on the people inside them. Although they didn't seem to notice that anything was happening to them, without exception they all began to grow long reddish-brown fur all over their bodies. The woman beside me acted as a translator once more, as she explained to me what was happening. Apparently, these people were those who didn't believe in God's Word, but rather relied on man's wisdom as truth. The woman told me that because they turned their backs on God, thinking themselves to be "too intelligent to need the crutch of religion", God was letting them go. *If they wanted to believe mankind came from apes, fine. He would let them become apes—making monkeys of them and their supposed wisdom.*

And then it became even more unsettling. As each person would finish turning into an ape-like thing, a bucket that looked like a silver milking pail would appear with him or her in the ball and begin bouncing off the top of the ape creature's head. "Ping. Ping. Ping", the buckets tapped. Next, the top of the hairy apes' heads flipped backwards, as though on a hinge, opening their mouths to receive what was in the bucket above them. One after another the silver pails tipped on their own, pouring what looked like buckets full of thick snot down the throats of the furry people. It was absolutely repulsive, and I heard the narrator woman explain that they were swallowing lies. It occurred to me that the hinge mouths were like what you would see a snake do when trying to swallow a rodent that was much bigger than itself. I turned to ask my guide if it was the father of lies (Satan) who was feeding them when I noticed she had stepped away from me, and now she was growing reddish-brown fur on her body! She wasn't in a plastic ball, but nevertheless, she too began to swallow the lies, and it startled me awake.

The next Sunday when I was at church, I saw Pastor Marty and asked him if he knew anything about a "Sky Mirror" and he had never heard of it. As I said, the detail and significance of this dream disturbed me enough to start investigating prophetic dreams further but until now, I haven't shared this with very many people because I didn't have the full revelation; I knew it wasn't the right time. Through the years since I had the dream, I have always felt that the mention of the Sky Mirror was an indication that whatever was to follow (in this case—the bucolic scene with the people in clear plastic spheres) would be seen from God's perspective. Yet I never had a clear indication of who my translator woman was. *We see similar characters who help interpret visions in Daniel and in Revelation but they are described as heavenly Spirit beings—elders, or perhaps angels.* A few months ago in the course of writing this book, it hit me. This woman represents the Believers in the church during the Last Days who fall for the lies! Despite all of the Biblical predictions of what would happen to the Church in the latter days, this year has been shocking to say the least. A number of church friends have become so fearful during Covid. They have bowed to the oppression of the constant news cycles and social media blasts and a strong fearful depression has left them paralyzed and ineffectual. Worse yet, we can see some churches have made so many compromises with the world, that their people have actually lost their way! WOE. Brothers and Sisters if this is you, it's not too late to turn back to Jesus—He IS the Way, the Truth, and the Life that you seek!

While Jesus walked on the earth, He also told stories. Why? Because while we may forget historical facts or how to solve a particular mathematical equation, human beings remember stories. Today, there are many people who have never read the Bible or given their life to Christ, yet who have heard of the Prodigal Son[xxxii] or the Good Samaritan[xxxiii]. While you might not remember much of anything that happened in your early childhood, I would bet most of you could tell me all about *the day you were born* as told to you by your parents. Stories matter. Stories of a life lived with Jesus matter most of all.

In a world where the biggest, loudest, and most technically savvy, plugged-in voices get heard, where money talks and corruption abounds, you might be tempted to think that your story isn't really important, or that it couldn't make a difference to anyone. **Don't listen to the lies**!! Jesus wanted me to write this FOR YOU. Now, it's Your turn.

Do you have a story from your own experience in which Jesus showed up for you? Maybe it was a miraculous healing, or some form of obvious protection from danger. Maybe it was a time He supernaturally provided more than you even knew you needed. Were you unexpectedly called into a mission field or was something that you believed hopelessly lost or broken actually restored? Are you learning to experience the fullness of life that Jesus came to give you? Let me encourage you, if nothing comes to mind, ask Him for the story He wants you to share! I promise you, it will be a GOOD one.

There is no life story too small—

Once when our family was on vacation in Maui and heading to an adventure that began before dawn, Abba taught me an important lesson. We were driving along the coast in our rental car, and I'm telling you, the darkness was so black we couldn't distinguish the ocean from the land, or the land from the sky. We're talking inky blackness. It was so dark my husband and I laughed out loud when we saw the sign for the photo op. vista. And then suddenly, a porchlight turned on several miles away, reaching us from what must have been a hill across a small bay. *One little light that broke through the darkness.*

There is no life story too common or redundant—

Time and again I've met people who put aside their dreams of speaking or writing or in some way sharing their experiences because other more well-known people are already saying essentially the same thing. This doesn't make your unique voice, your unique approach any less important! There is a reason God used so many different voices in His Word to give the same message. There's a reason why people with the same faith are drawn to different pastors. Though they're giving the same message, we tend to listen and understand best from someone who speaks our language; these are pastors and teachers with whom we share a more similar worldview based on age, background, style or personality. *Whether it be one person at a time or a huge online platform, trust that the Lord will bring you the audience who will best hear from YOU.*

Friend, God appointed You for this significant moment in history—HIS Story. We don't need to be fearful; we already have a roadmap of what's coming. The time has ended for His children to sit on the sidelines and wish for yesterday to return. When we're honest with ourselves, yesterday wasn't that great. Our HOPE is in the future and our Joy is in getting to partner with Him to point to the abundant LIFE we have with Jesus with everyone He puts in our path!!

> The LORD bless you
> and keep you;
> the LORD make his face shine on you
> and be gracious to you;
> the LORD turn his face toward you
> and give you peace. (Num 6:24-26 NIV)

And may you all LIVE Happily Ever After

REFERENCES

Opening
[i] To Kill a Mockingbird, Harper Lee ©1960
Charlotte's Web, E.B. White ©1952
[ii] Left Behind, Series by Tim LaHaye and Jerry B. Jenkins © 1995- 2007
[iii] "Live Like You Were Dying", Tim McGraw 2004
[iv] Mere Christianity, C.S. Lewis © 1952
[v] The Case for Christ, Lee Stroble © 1998

Chapter 1
[vi] Eph 3:18 NLT

Chapter 2
[vii] John 3:16
[viii] This portion of what I call my "Walking Miracle Story" has been partially recaptured from my book, Going Deeper ©2014

Chapter 3
[ix] Acts 2:17
[x] The Veil, Blake K. Healy ©2012

Chapter 4
[xi] Malachi 3:10

Chapter 5
[xii] Proverbs 31:25 NLT

Chapter 6
[xiii] Phil 4:8-9
[xiv] Change Your Life Daily Bible, Becky Tirabassi Resources ©1996
[xv] 1 Cor 12:18-23

xvi   Jesus Calling, Sarah Young ©2004
xvii   The Book of Mysteries, Jonathan Cahn ©2016
xviii II Cor 5:17
xix   1 Peter 2:9
xx   Psalms 37:4
xxi   "Who You Say I Am" Hillsong Worship 2018
xxii   Sacred Pathways, Gary Thomas ©1996

Chapter 7

xxiii   "Goodness of God" Bethel Music and Jenn Johnson 2019
xxiv   Mark 2:1-12
xxv   James 3:2-12
xxvi   Luke 11:25-31
xxvii   Eph 6:11-18
xxviii "Fragrance to Fire" Dunsin Oyekan 2020
xxix   2 Tim 4:18
xxx   "No More Fear- The Roadtrip Story," has been recaptured from my blog: www.SparkTwinkleShine.wordpress.com, posted Jan 15, 2020

Closing

xxxi   1 Cor 3:19
xxxii   Luke 15:11-32
xxxiii Luke 10:30-37

ABOUT THE AUTHOR

At 32, Cara Walter said "Yes!" to Jesus, beginning a journey of faith where she has experienced more Joy, Peace, and Love than she ever thought possible! As a speaker and writer, Cara encourages others with inspiring stories of His Abundant Life.

She is also the author of *Going Deeper-Building an Intimate Walk with the Spirit of God.*

Cara lives with her husband in McKinney, Texas, where she is joyfully following the Lord's leading in this new chapter.

www.carawalter.com

Printed in the United States
By Bookmasters